SOBER

"Don't lose your HEAD"

Pastor Samuel Saint Louis

"Most of us were born into this world headfirst, emerging from the womb. Similarly, to escape from challenging circumstances, professional limitations, or stagnation in your ministry, you need to lead with your head. Don't lose your mind."

A General perspective on Sobriety, mental Health and Spiritual Growth

Dedication

This is dedicated to the God Father, Jesus the Son and the Holy Spirit. To my wife Sherly V. Saint Louis without her I would never make it. and also, to my children Israel and Salomon Saint Louis. It is also in dedication to my father Renold Saint Louis and my mother Marie D. Saint Louis a strong and supportive woman. It dedicated to my pastor Ernst Joseph a coach, a mentor, a father. To all my church members all over the world.

PREFACES

If we forged a list of all the world is made of, we would stand in awe at the layers of complexity and fascination that surround us. The course of nature has been set by the master Creator who spoke our world and all the universes into existence. His incredible blueprint is filled with intricacies that keep our world spinning on its proper path. He is the God of order and has set the perfect example for us to follow.

If God had haphazardly thrown His impeccable creation together, it would not be awe-inspiring or marvelous. Instead, severe chaos would ensue. It is safe to say, backed by the Word of God, that our Creator designed his masterpiece of creation with all seriousness. Even when the time came to present a spotless Lamb to take away the sins of the world, God's plan was specific and perfect.

And here *we* are.

While man cannot attain complete perfection in this earthly body, God gave us a model of excellence to follow. Wise men realize accomplishing great things will happen when focus and goals are set in place with a sober mind.

Consider this list of objects, positions, and organizations:

- head of the body

- head of the country

- head of state

- head of security

- head of the baby at birth

- head of household

- head of the church

- headquarters

- warhead

All of the subjects above play important parts in many different areas of life.

Without the head on a body or the head of a baby at birth, life cannot survive.

Without the head of a country and the head of a state, confusion and chaos will take over, most likely causing many casualties of innocent life.

Without a warhead, a missile would be rendered useless.

The head is the focus in many areas. Rightfully so because without it, order will dissolve. In order for the head to continually work at peak performance, the utmost care and protection are necessary.

While this is important in natural areas of life and society, this is *critical* in our spiritual walk.

Ephesians 6:13-17 tells us, *"Therefore take up the whole armor of God, that you may be able to withstand in the evil* *day, and having done all, to stand firm. Stand therefore, having fastened on the belt of truth, and having put on the breastplate of righteousness, and, as shoes for your feet, having put on the readiness given by the gospel of peace. In all circumstances take up the shield of faith, with which you can extinguish all the flaming darts of the evil one; and take the helmet of salvation, and the sword of the Spirit, which is the word of God,"*

We can have truth, live a moral lifestyle, offer the gospel of peace to others, and practice faith in God, but if we fail to wear the helmet of salvation, the head is not protected. It is absolutely foolish to leave the head -our minds- unguarded. To do so threatens the loss of our head, and if we lose that, we will lose everything.

In our natural lives, helmets and hard hats are non-negotiable gear for certain jobs. If a blow to the head is hard enough, a brain injury can occur. Many times, the damage cannot be reversed.

Spiritually speaking, the head must be strongly guarded as well. Those who are in positions to make a difference in the lives of others are often a target for being attacked. Similar to the example of receiving a heavy blow in the natural body, a hard hit to a leader can be devastating enough to destroy him or her.

Whether we carry a title of leadership or not, our lives are meant to impact and influence others around us, as we fill the great commission of sharing the gospel. Above all we set out to do for Jesus, and all we strive to accomplish in our Christian walk, protecting our minds cannot be emphasized enough.

At our birth, most of us came out from the womb head first. Our place of darkness was replaced with light and clarity. In order to come out of darkness when our minds are bombarded with bad situations, stagnation in ministry, and other frustrating, challenging times, the head must come out of that dark place first.

We must set aside the heavy weights that are clouding our thoughts and regain focus to protect our minds. We can start by giving our needs to God.

Philippians 4:6-7 tells us, *"Do not be anxious about anything, but in everything by prayer and supplication with thanksgiving let your requests be made known to God. And the peace of God, which surpasses all understanding, will guard your hearts and your minds in Christ Jesus."*

Did our Lord not come to set us free and give us a more abundant life? If problems are permitted to rein in our minds instead of allowing God that place of honor, the hardships of life will hold us in bondage forever. If we lose our minds to a mountain of thoughts that revolve around sickness, bills, debts, problems, fears, grudges, bitterness, and more, we will lack the ability to gain clear focus on what needs to be done to make our situations better and our spiritual walk healthy once again. Stepping back for a clear view of our situations will help us gain clarity for the actions we need to take.

The Word will help us walk according to the Spirit with sober-mindedness and not according to our flesh. 1 Peter 5:8 shares a serious reminder, telling us to, *"Be sober-minded; be watchful. Your adversary the devil prowls around like a roaring lion, seeking someone to devour."*

The enemy who waits for the perfect opportunity to pounce has few chances of catching us off-guard when we are sober-minded and make diligent efforts to keep our minds protected. What can you do?

Pray without ceasing.

Read the Word and hide it in your heart.

Stand firm in your faith.

Lean on Jesus and rely on His strength when your own is fading.

Embrace the principles of God and let His Word guide you.

Be cautious about your choices of music, reading material, entertainment, and ungodly friendships.

Surround yourself with those who aim to sharpen, encourage, and pray for you.

Put on the <u>whole</u> armor of God.

When the importance of protecting our minds is taken seriously, the potential and ability to do and see more than we've ever imagined become a possibility.

What could be greater than that?

That potential and ability becoming a probability!

TABLE OF CONTENTS

INTRODUCTION

Sobriety is a state of being free from the influence of intoxicating substances or harmful behaviors, promoting self-control, rationality, and calmness in all areas of life. In several places throughout the New Testament, being sober-minded is encouraged, emphasizing the importance of avoiding any influence that may lead us astray from sound judgment. For church leaders and their spouses, being sober-minded is a unique qualification, signifying reverence for their responsibility as representatives of Christ.

Chapter one of this book discusses the reasons for sobriety, highlighting the positive changes it can bring to one's life, especially for those struggling with addiction. It also stresses the need for understanding the complexities involved in achieving recovery and taking the necessary steps to overcome addiction.

Chapter two emphasizes that disappointment and trials are inevitable in life, but we can choose not to become discouraged by them. God's plans for us are sure, true, and faithful, and we can trust in His faithfulness to execute those plans in our lives. The author believes that God's plan extends to all aspects of life, and we should continually have faith and belief in God's plan for our lives. It also highlights the importance of having goals, planning, strategizing, and executing action plans to achieve success in life. However, it is important to remember that our plans are based on our limited knowledge, and they may change as our interests or circumstances change.

Chapter three reveals God's intention for our lives is a topic of great importance for those who seek to understand the meaning of their existence. According to the Bible, God's intention encompasses all aspects of our lives, including physical, mental, and spiritual well-being. In 3 John 2, it is written that God wishes for us to prosper and be in good health, just as our soul prospers. This verse reveals that God's intentions for our lives include material and financial prosperity, physical and mental health, and spiritual growth. In this chapter, we will explore these three aspects of God's intentions and learn how we can apply His principles to our lives.

Chapter four talk about the helmet of salvation is a metaphorical piece of armor mentioned in Ephesians 6:17, which represents the assurance of salvation that protects us from the attacks of the enemy. Just like a Roman helmet, which protected the head of a soldier from the blows of the enemy, the helmet of salvation protects our minds from the attacks of Satan. The helmet is the last piece of armor to be put on before battle, signifying the final act of readiness before combat. It is essential for survival because it protects the brain, which controls the decisions and reactions of the rest of the body. The helmet of salvation represents the ongoing, eternal state of deliverance that Christians enjoy in the present.

INTRODUCTION

Chapter five is about the concept that involves recognizing and appreciating diversity, managing differences, and solving puzzles to achieve a mentally effective and mature mindset. Diversity is the key to our strength, intelligence, and innovation, but it can also lead to misunderstanding and confusion if not managed effectively. The same Spirit is the source of all diversity, which should be appreciated and celebrated. Apostle Paul, in his letters to the Corinthians, emphasized that conformity is not necessary for unity. Instead, the Lordship of Jesus is necessary for unity, and the Holy Spirit energizes unity and enables the edification of the Body. The scripture encourages us to have a sound mind, which entails understanding and ascribing mental capacities to others, and labeling entities as good or bad, or actions as right or wrong.

Chapter six renewing the mind is a process that involves changing our thought patterns and aligning them with God's thoughts and ways. This transformation is achieved through the power of the Holy Spirit, who helps us to understand God's will and purpose for our lives. It involves replacing negative and destructive thoughts with positive and constructive ones, as well as letting go of old ways of thinking that do not align with God's truth.

Chapter seven went further to discusses the importance of hope in strengthening the mind and how the definition of hope can vary from person to person. It highlights that not all thoughts should be believed, and the mind can be deceived by sin, including self-deception, and

Satan's lies. The chapter stresses the importance of questioning our thoughts and not blindly accepting them. It also mentions that the Bible provides several principles for renewing and submitting our thoughts to control them.

Chapter eight reflects on the power of meditation lies in its ability to focus our minds on a specific idea or thing. Biblical meditation is different from the meditation taught in Far Eastern religions, as it encourages us to fill our minds with God's Word instead of emptying them. When we meditate on God's Word and promises, we create a "sound" in our minds that impacts the direction of our choices and experiences. Whatever we meditate on long enough will try to control our thinking, and eventually become our reality. Therefore, it's crucial to develop the right meditations and replace negative imaginations with focused prayer requests. Worry is the practice of negative meditation, and it destroys faith and keeps us trapped in fear and avoidance. By bringing our fears and problems to God in prayer, we can take action and trust in His plans and possibilities for our lives.

Chapter nine; sobriety is a concept that has been emphasized throughout history as a crucial aspect of personal well-being and spiritual development. In the Bible, sobriety is presented as a state of being free from all forms of intoxication, whether physical or spiritual. This is reflected in various passages that urge people to be mentally prepared, alert, and free from addiction to alcohol. However, the question of whether it is permissible for Christians to consume alcohol remains a topic of debate. In this text, we

INTRODUCTION

will explore the concept of sobriety in the Bible, the effects of alcohol on the body and mind, and the role of alcohol in Christian life.

In conclusion, the message of God's love and purpose for humanity is one that has been shared throughout the ages. It is a message of peace and life, and it is available to all who are willing to receive it. However, our disobedience and sin have caused a separation between us and God, leading to death and despair. Human attempts to bridge this gap have failed time and time again, but there is hope. God's remedy is found in the person of Jesus Christ, who died on the cross to pay the penalty for our sins and bring us back into relationship with God. We must respond by receiving Christ into our lives through faith and repentance, and by doing so, we are assured of eternal life with Him. The Bible tells us that we are saved by grace through faith, and that this gift of salvation is available to all who believe in the name of the Son of God. May this message of hope and salvation be received by all who hear it.

CHAPTER ONE

SOBRIETY

Arthur Ashe once said, "True heroism is remarkably sober, very non-dramatic. It is not the urge to surpass all others at whatever cost, but the urge to serve others at whatever cost." The concept of being sober-minded appears in several places throughout the New Testament, such as 1 Peter 4:7, 5:8, Titus 2:2, 6, and 1 Corinthians 15:34. In 2 Timothy 4:5, Paul instructs Timothy to be "sober-minded, endure suffering, do the work of an evangelist, fulfill your ministry" (ESV). The term sober-minded means "free from intoxicating influences," indicating an individual who is not under the control of dangerous outside forces, such as alcohol or drugs.

Being sober-minded goes beyond avoiding intoxicating substances; it means not being captivated by any influence that may lead us astray from sound judgment. The sober-minded individual is figuratively "unintoxicated," demonstrating self-control, rationality, and calmness in all areas of life. Other translations of 2 Timothy 4:5 instruct Timothy to "keep your head" (NIV), "keep a clear mind" (NLT), and "exercise self-control" (CSB). Being sober-minded is a unique qualification for church leaders and their spouses (1 Timothy 3:2, 11; Titus 1:8), who should be reverentially aware of their responsibility as representatives of Christ (2

Corinthians 5:20). Peter urged believers to "be self-controlled and sober-minded for the sake of your prayers" (1 Peter 4:7, ESV) as the end of all things draws near. Those who are sober-minded will recognize the importance of prayer and take the opportunity to pray at every appropriate moment.

More often than not, we witness the opposite of sober-mindedness displayed in our world: stupidity, irresponsible choices, foolish experimentation with harmful substances or behaviors, and crude joking. These actions are in direct opposition to the command to be sober-minded. Ephesians 5:3–4 lists behaviors that conflict with sober-minded living, stating, "But fornication, and all uncleanness, or covetousness, let it not be once named among you, as becometh saints; Neither filthiness, nor foolish talking, nor jesting, which are not convenient." Just in case someone may think that this is merely an inventory of judgmental preferences, Paul continues by writing, "For this ye know, that no whoremonger, nor unclean person, nor covetous man, who is an idolater, hath any inheritance in the kingdom of Christ and of God. Let no man deceive you with vain words: for because of these things cometh the wrath of God upon the children of disobedience. Be not ye therefore partakers with them" (Ephesians 5:5–7).

Being sober-minded does not mean living a sour, joyless existence. In fact, sober-minded Christians are to be filled with the enjoyment of the Holy Ghost continually. Eliminating foolishness, frivolity, and mind-numbing silliness from our lives allows us to focus on what is real, eternal, and inspiring. Jesus' command to His sleepy-headed disciples highlights the necessity of sober-mindedness: "Watch and pray so that you will not fall into temptation" (Mark 14:38).

Ephesians 5:18 instructs us to avoid being filled with wine, which leads to debauchery, but rather to be continually filled with the Holy Ghost. This verse implies that we can only choose one of these options, but not both. If we pursue drunkenness, we cannot also pursue God. If substances control us, we cannot be controlled by the Holy Ghost. Sober-minded people choose to abstain from practices that might lead them into sin.

In Romans 13:12–14, Paul explains the importance behind the frequent commands to be sober-minded: "The night is far spent, the day is at hand: let us therefore cast off the works of darkness, and let us put on the armour of light. Let us walk honestly, as in the day; not in rioting and drunkenness, not in chambering and wantonness, not in strife and envying. But put ye on the Lord Jesus Christ, and make not provision for the flesh, to fulfill the lusts thereof." which may be a good description of being sober-minded.

REASONS FOR SOBRIETY FOR ADDICTS

Many people turn to alcohol to suppress their problems, but an African proverb teaches that alcohol can only provide temporary relief and cannot erase the underlying issues. The most advisable and effective way to deal with difficult problems is to face them head-on, which is best achieved through sobriety. The prospect of being sober can be scary for many people. Much of our social behavior revolves around the use of drugs in one form or another. Even if you are not an addict, living a sober lifestyle can seem like a challenging task. However, giving up drinking or drugs can lead to positive changes in your life in a multitude of ways, whether you are trying to overcome addiction or simply looking to improve your health.

Acknowledging the need to get sober is one thing; understanding how to go about it is entirely another. While recognizing the problem is half the battle, there is still another half to follow if the person wants to successfully manage the issue and achieve recovery. It can be intimidating to know what steps to take to become sober. Some individuals might look for a quick fix without understanding the complexities involved in overcoming addiction. Others may be halted in their tracks by not knowing what to do first. In either case, it's easy to get lost along the way if the person isn't aware of the potential complications and the tools and resources that can help overcome those challenges. With a guide that outlines the various steps required to support the entire journey, the path to addiction recovery can be more straightforward, less frightening, and more likely to result in a positive outcome. Below are some reasons to consider getting sober.

SOBRIETY

1. You sleep better.

The significance of good sleep cannot be emphasized enough. When you are deprived of sleep, you feel irritable, unfocused, and unwell. Alcohol and drugs are not conducive to good sleep - they can keep you up late at night, make it difficult to fall asleep when you want to, or cause daytime sleepiness. When you are sober, you can maintain a healthy sleep schedule and wake up feeling refreshed every day.

2. Your diet improves.

When you are under the influence, it is all too easy to give in to cravings for greasy, sweet, or salty foods. It is much easier to eat healthily when you are sober. You experience fewer cravings, and you are not surrounded by temptations like bar food.

3. Your weight stabilizes.

It is effortless to consume a large number of empty calories with just a few drinks. When you combine the calories in alcohol with the aforementioned food cravings, you have a recipe for weight gain. When you are sober, you will likely find that you stop gaining weight (and perhaps even lose a few pounds) without really making an effort.

4. You avoid alcohol- or drug-related health problems.

Nobody likes to think that they could find themselves with a disease or other substance-related health problems. However, people are diagnosed with these diseases every day, and if you regularly abuse alcohol or drugs, the likelihood is high that you'll eventually be one of them. When you're sober, you don't have to worry about developing life-threatening complications from your habits.

5. You've got more free time.

Drinking and using drugs can consume a lot of your time and energy. You have to spend time acquiring your substance of choice, using it, and then recovering from its effects. Sobriety gives all that time back to you. You can use it to work on your hobbies, learn new skills, spend time with your loved ones, work out, or do anything else you please.

6. You've got extra money.

Alcohol and drugs can be expensive. It's much easier to stay financially fit when you're sober. Besides saving all that money in the first place, you'll be in a better state of mind to make good financial decisions. Having that extra cash opens up a whole world of new opportunities - you can choose to buy a house, take a vacation, or go back to school, for instance.

7. Your relationships get stronger.

When you're sober, you have more time and mental energy to spend on the people who matter most to you. Without the distraction of wondering when you can go get drunk or high, you'll be able to stay physically and emotionally present with others. You'll probably discover that the important relationships in your life mean much more to you than drugs or alcohol ever did.

8. You get sick less often.

Alcohol and drugs can be detrimental to your health. When you don't consume anything unhealthy, you won't be as susceptible to colds and stomach bugs.

9. Your memory improves.

Have you ever woken up unable to recall what happened the night before? It's a little unsettling. Even if you don't tend to black out under the influence, alcohol and drugs can make your memory foggy and unreliable. When you're sober, you'll feel sharper and more alert, and you'll be able to remember things more clearly.

10. You've got more energy.

Regular use of alcohol and drugs can take a toll on your body and disrupt your sleep, leaving you feeling pretty bad. Quitting these substances can instantly make you feel years younger. You won't have to nurse hangovers or take afternoon naps to get through the day anymore.

11. You're more productive.

It's not hard to see why people are more productive when they're sober. When you have high energy levels and a lot of free time, it's easier to stay focused on work, school, and personal projects.

12. You've got more fun.

It might sound counterintuitive, but drinking or using drugs really isn't that enjoyable. Sure, being intoxicated might feel good for a short time, but are you truly having fun? Being sober allows you to push your boundaries and celebrate in ways that aren't possible when you're drunk or high. You can visit new places, try new things, and be fully present in your life – and that's always more fulfilling than relying on a drink.

13. You'll find healthy ways to affect problems.

The basic disease model of addiction suggests that many people use drugs or alcohol to cope with their problems. If this sounds like you, you might be surprised to find out how much more effectively you can handle things sober. It may feel like drinking or using drugs makes your problems disappear, but as anyone who has struggled with addiction knows, this is just an illusion. When you commit to sobriety, you can actually solve your problems instead of ignoring them.

14. You rebuild your self-image.

How do you feel about yourself when you're drinking or using drugs? Do you respect yourself and your decisions? Maybe not, especially if your substance use has become problematic. Getting and staying sober can change the way you see yourself. You won't have to think of yourself as a person with no self-control or someone who says foolish things when intoxicated. Additionally, affirming your decision to remain sober can boost your self-esteem.

ADDICTION RELAPSE

Addiction relapse is a common occurrence in the management of chronic diseases. Addiction, much like asthma, diabetes, and hypertension, is a chronic condition that requires treatment. There are many individuals who desire to achieve sobriety but experience intense cravings and eventually return to using their substance of choice.

However, this does not necessarily mean that the treatment for addiction is ineffective. Relapse is a possibility for many individuals who are striving to overcome addiction. If you find yourself in this situation, it is important to prepare yourself for how to recover from a relapse, forgive yourself, and return to your treatment program.

However, it is crucial not to use relapse as an excuse to revert to drug or alcohol use. Doing so will only trap you in an endless cycle, leading to frustration and a lack of progress in your treatment. It is important to take responsibility for your actions and make necessary adjustments to your lifestyle in order to move forward and recover from addiction.

Why Does Relapse Happen?

Usually, people recovering from addiction to illicit substances often relapse because they are triggered by certain factors, such as being in places where they previously used drugs or seeing drug paraphernalia.

These triggers can vary from person to person. Exposure to specific places, things, or people can cause intense cravings to use drugs or alcohol. However, during recovery, individuals can learn how to manage these triggers through various therapy sessions.

Taking the initiative to get sober is the first step toward recovery. It's crucial to recognize within yourself that you want to improve. However, relying solely on willpower is not enough to get you through the process. Recovery requires a great deal of practice and your full commitment.

In the event of a relapse, it's important not to view yourself as a failure or believe that all your hard work has gone to waste. As a brain disease, addiction can cause individuals in recovery to engage in compulsive behavior, even if they understand the negative consequences they may face.

What are the various Factors that Cause a Relapse?

Once you have completed the treatment program at a rehabilitation center, it does not automatically guarantee sobriety. However, you are now equipped with the knowledge and skills to work towards becoming clean and sober. The real work begins when you return home and face the familiar environments where you used to use drugs. Exposure to these environments can trigger memories that induce the urge to use drugs, which is a common cause of addiction relapse. Let's take a look at other factors that can lead to relapse.

Triggers

As we discussed earlier, triggers can be anything such as people, situations, emotions, thoughts, or feelings that remind you of your previous habits and can lead you back to using drugs or drinking. For example, you may simply walk past the familiar pub where you used to drink, and suddenly feel triggered by cravings to go inside and have a few drinks.

Triggers can also arise when you attend social gatherings where alcoholic beverages are available. They can also manifest when you feel sad, stressed, or have trouble sleeping. In such situations, you may feel that by taking the substance, you would feel better again. This is because you have become accustomed to using it to relax and deal with your problems.

Additionally, if you keep in touch with individuals whom you want to consume drugs with, there is a high probability that you may relapse. They could coerce you into having a few drinks or taking a small amount of drugs, claiming that it won't affect your recovery. However, in reality, these substances can draw you back into the habit of being a heavy user.

SOBER

Not Seeking Aftercare

For many individuals who successfully complete rehab, sticking to the treatment plan and aftercare can be challenging. It's common to think that their time in the rehab center has cured them of their addiction. However, going to rehab is not a guarantee that there won't be a relapse. It's crucial to continue taking the necessary steps to maintain sobriety and remain drug-free.

Aftercare services are provided to individuals after completing their treatment program in the rehab center. These services include psychotherapy sessions and other programs designed to help prevent relapse. You'll also receive guidance on how to avoid triggers that could lead to a relapse. That's why seeking aftercare treatment is essential once your rehab program is over.

Sober housing can also be a part of the aftercare program. It provides individuals with substance-free homes where they can live with others who are also recovering from addiction. This type of living environment offers a supportive community where residents can help each other successfully abstain from using drugs or alcohol.

Other Factors to observe

Relapse can be caused by both external and internal factors. It's important to be aware of these factors as experiencing relapse can delay your recovery from addiction.

Let's take a look at some of the things that can contribute to relapse.

Exhaustion or fatigue can affect your daily functioning. If you're dealing with a lot of stress, it may create urges to revert back to your bad habits in order to numb the psychological or physical pain you're experiencing. If you have depression, it's important to be cautious of how you react to it during a depressive episode. Depression is a mental health condition that often co-occurs with addiction to drugs or alcohol.

During a depressive episode, you may experience oversleeping, difficulty concentrating, and a loss of interest in activities that once brought you joy. It's natural to believe that drugs or alcohol may provide some relief from these symptoms. However, the reality is that substance abuse will only exacerbate the situation and make things worse.

How to recover from a Relapse?

Addiction treatment is only the beginning. If you've completed a program for your treatment, that's already a significant step. However, you should also be prepared for the real world outside of the rehabilitation center. When you return to your usual setting, you'll be exposed to triggers that could lead you back to your old habits.

In a scenario, your colleagues at work may invite you out on a Friday night, insisting that one drink won't hurt. You may be convinced and decide to join them, but the next thing you know, you're in the hospital because you consumed too much alcohol and couldn't control yourself. It's important to understand that addiction is a disease, and no amount of willpower will be enough to make you stop using drugs or alcohol. Even if you're aware of the negative consequences of substance use, you may still struggle to resist the urge to use.

What you need to know is that addiction can be a disease, and you should avoid exposing yourself to triggers until you have the necessary knowledge and skills to deal with them effectively. Simply put, you may feel the urge to use drugs or alcohol repeatedly, but at the very least, you should learn how to avoid exposure. Do not put yourself in a situation where you may be tempted to return to your bad habits.

Although relapse is common, it does not mean that you should simply give in to temptation without a good fight. Triggers and temptations will arise, and you need to be prepared to deal with them. Here are some tips we have prepared for you:

Be Ready

Many recovering addicts feel extreme shame, humiliation, and guilt when they experience a relapse. If this happens to you, it's important to allow yourself to feel these emotions. However, instead of wallowing in them, use them as motivation to return to your treatment program. Do not allow negativity to pull you down, and remember that experiencing a relapse does not make you a failure.

Get the Much-Needed Support

If you have recently completed your treatment at a rehab center, or have been sober for a few weeks or months and experience a relapse, it is important to schedule a meeting with your counselor.

During this session, you need to be prepared for a difficult conversation, as you will have to admit that you made a mistake. It can be hard and humbling to admit that you had a moment of weakness and were unable to control your cravings, even if you tried very hard. Always remember that addiction is a disease, and you cannot fully control everything.

That's why meeting with an addiction counselor is crucial, as it allows you to express how you are feeling after experiencing a relapse. During the session, you can process feelings of shame and guilt, and learn how to handle difficult times and avoid relapse in the future.

Call Your Family or Friends

Taking this step can be difficult, especially if your addiction has caused you to burn some bridges along the way. However, it is important to acknowledge that support from family and friends is crucial if you want to succeed in your recovery.

If you ever feel like you are about to give in to your cravings, call up your support system and tell them how you are feeling. Let them know how difficult it is to resist the urge to take drugs or drink alcohol. By talking to them, you can express your frustrations and they can offer their support by reminding you of your goals and why you are trying to get sober.

Your family and close friends love and care about you. Even if you experience a relapse, if they see that you are sincere about getting back on track with your recovery, they will always support you and hope for the best for you in your journey towards overcoming addiction.

Think About Going Back to Treatment

The decision to go back to treatment will depend on the severity of your relapse. For example, if your relapse was limited to just one night of drinking or using drugs, then it is possible that you may be able to resume your recovery without encountering significant challenges.

However, if you have been drinking or using drugs for several weeks now, then it may be time to consider going back to treatment. Keep in mind that addiction and recovery experiences are unique to each individual. There are many treatment centers that offer aftercare services, so take full advantage of them as you will need all the help and support that you can get. Consult with your addiction counselor and ask questions on how you can better equip yourself to prevent relapse.

Challenge Yourself

Whenever you experience a relapse, avoid thinking of it as a failure or perceiving yourself as a failure. Instead, challenge yourself to move past that episode. Remember all the times you were sober and celebrate those achievements.

Regarding your relapse event, try to learn as much as possible from it. What were the triggers? Identify them and make a list. Tell yourself that you should avoid those triggers in the future. How did the relapse make you feel afterward? It probably felt terrible. Remind yourself that you don't want to find yourself in that position again. Challenge yourself to move past the negativity and continue with your addiction recovery journey.

Stay Positive

Experiencing a relapse can be disappointing, but don't be too hard on yourself. The relapse has already happened, and there's nothing you can do about it. Instead of dwelling on negative feelings, remind yourself that you can at least learn from the experience.

SOBER

Tell yourself, "Now I know better." Every step you take towards recovery, including the relapse, is a breakthrough. As long as you resist the temptations of your past life, you're still doing well and making progress in your recovery journey. Stay positive and keep working towards your goal!

A thoughtful act can be a wise act. Many people become overwhelmed with the challenges of life and allow their circumstances to dictate their actions, rather than taking control themselves. When we are unable to see past our struggles, we tend to dwell on them, which can lead to addiction as we attempt to escape our problems.

However, it is important to remember that there is likely someone who has experienced a similar ordeal before us. We can learn from their experiences and gain valuable insights on how to manage our own predicament. By doing so, we can overcome our challenges and emerge stronger.

Furthermore, it is important to ask ourselves whether there are any available resources that we can utilize to help us tackle the situation at hand. By being resourceful, we can find solutions and make progress, rather than becoming stagnant and overwhelmed.

Someone once told me that only a thoughtless mind would resort to drinking. While alcohol and other stimulants have the potential to take one's mind and thoughts far away from prevailing situations, they only succeed in temporarily masking the pain. Eventually, the entire situation will resurface, sometimes even worse than before. There are ways around the situation if you take the time to think it through. Thinking before acting may be a sign of maturity.

At times, things can be so perplexing that one might not be able to think straight. This is where the importance of having genuine and wise friends comes in. The company we keep matters, especially when we are feeling down. The advice and counsel of our friends have the potential to either weaken or strengthen us in life. So, it's important to surround ourselves with good friends who can lift us up when we need it. With good friends by our side, we can keep moving forward.

CHAPTER TWO

GOD'S PLAN

Charles Stanley once said, "Disappointment is inevitable. But to become discouraged, there's a choice I make. God would never discourage me. He would always point me to himself and ask me to trust him. Therefore, my discouragement is from Satan. As you go through the emotions that we have, hostility, bitterness, unforgiveness, all of these are attacks from Satan." Isaac Bashevis Singer put it in another way, "Life is God's novel. Let him write it." From the Scriptures, Jeremiah 29:11 says, "For I know the thoughts that I think toward you, saith the LORD, thoughts of peace, and not of evil, to give you an expected end." God has a purpose and a plan for you. His plans are sure, true, and faithful. This doesn't mean that you will never experience problems or trials in life, but you do have an endless future in Christ spiritually. God's plan for you is to prosper and grow spiritually in Christ within the very situation you are in right now. God's plans for you are sure, and they are great.

Although this chapter primarily focuses on the scriptural perspective of God's plan and faithfulness to its fulfillment, it also presents the idea that God's purpose for us extends to all aspects of life. No matter how we approach it, there is a reflection of God's plan in all facets of life, such as business, entrepreneurship, finance, family, academics, marriage, physical and mental health, society, and any other sphere of influence. In essence, every aspect of our lives can be viewed in the context of God's plan for us.

What does it take to be successful in life? Having a goal is a good starting point, but it takes much more than that. It requires research and generating findings about the goals, planning, strategizing, and working, executing the action plans, obtaining results, and then replanning for better results. These steps are crucial for achieving success in life. However, it is important to remember that we must believe in ourselves and be faithful to executing what we plan for success.

The same principle applies to God's plan for our lives. God has a plan for each one of us, and He is dutifully working out His plans. Therefore, there is no need to worry or be anxious. If God can plan all the facets of the world - the earth, sun, moon, stars, water bodies, and all life forms, including humans and animals of different sizes and shapes - and all these creations are well-perfected, then His plan for our lives must be perfect too. Keeping this in mind will help us trust and rely on His faithfulness for our lives. No matter the situation in life, there is always hope, and there is light at the end of the tunnel.

Continual faith and belief in God are essential, and we should dig deep into God's plan for our lives.

GOD'S PLAN

GOD'S PLANS FOR YOU TRUE AND FAITHFUL

We all make plans for the long term in our lives, don't we? However, not all of our plans turn out the way we want them to. We can be influenced by people, circumstances, and opportunities, and our choices, both good and bad, can affect whether we succeed with our plans or not. It's important to note that the plans we make are based on our limited knowledge and sometimes with self-interest in mind. As a result, they may change as our interests or circumstances change.

This is what the Lord Almighty, the God of Israel, says to all those whom I carried into exile from Jerusalem to Babylon: 'Build houses and settle down; plant gardens and eat what they produce. Marry and have sons and daughters; find wives for your sons and give your daughters in marriage, so that they too may have sons and daughters. Increase in number; do not decrease. Also, seek the peace and prosperity of the city to which I have carried you into exile. Pray to the Lord for it, because if it prospers, you too will prosper.' Yes, this is what the Lord Almighty, the God of Israel, says: 'Do not let the prophets and diviners among you deceive you. Do not listen to the dreams you encourage them to have. They are prophesying lies to you in my name. I have not sent them,' declares the Lord. This is what the Lord says: 'When seventy years are completed for Babylon, I will come to you and fulfill my good promise to bring you back to this place. For I know the plans I have for you,' declares the Lord, 'plans to prosper you and not to harm you, plans to give you hope and a future. Then you will call on me and come and pray to me, and I will listen to you. You will seek me and find me when you seek me with all your heart. I will be found by you,' declares the Lord, 'and will bring you back from captivity. I will gather you from all the nations and places where I have banished you,' declares the Lord, 'and will bring you back to the place from which I carried you into exile.' (Jeremiah 29:4-14, NIV)."

God's plans for you are certain and unchanging. His plans for you are great, and the choices you make can impact your future. Just like Israel, no matter what plans they had or choices they made, God's plan for them remained constant and unwavering. His plan was certain.

God utilized Nebuchadnezzar to create a situation in the lives of the Israelites that would bring them to a point of repentance and crying out to God once again. God used their time in Babylon for their benefit so that they would turn back to Him. It's important to remember that rebellion and sin have consequences.

Both the Old and New Testaments reveal God's love and promise of hope and a future for those who are faithful and call upon the Lord. Although God doesn't prevent us from making bad decisions and turning our backs on Him, He never turns His back on us permanently. God's plan for us is never to harm us, but rather to give us hope and a bright future. This hope and future are available to all who seek God and turn to His name.

GOD'S PLAN

Nobody knows what the future holds, and we all make plans without certainty of what tomorrow will bring. However, this doesn't mean we should avoid making plans. Instead, we should consider our plans in light of God's plan for our lives. The plans we make and the decisions others make can have a significant impact on our future. The truth is that our plans may face obstacles due to unforeseen events, mistakes, or choices to rebel and sin. But these roadblocks, bondage, or spiritual exiles may be God's way of getting our attention and leading us to reconsider our plans, and to turn back to the Lord and His plan for our lives.

What plans have you made for your life? Are they going as planned? Have you taken into consideration God's plan for your life? It's important to remember where you came from and where you're headed. Take some time to reflect on where your plans are taking you in comparison to what God desires for you. The Bible says, 'But remember the Lord your God, for it is he who gives you the ability to produce wealth, and so confirms his covenant, which he swore to your ancestors, as it is today.' (Deuteronomy 8:18) I believe that the Israelites, and people today, do not intentionally forget the Lord. However, sin and selfish desires can cloud our hearts and spiritual vision. The truth is, due to the Israelites' choices and rebellion against God, He allowed other nations to take them captive. The time of captivity and exile that the Israelites experienced was not meant to harm or destroy them; but rather to place them in a position where they would lift their eyes to heaven and seek God once again.

Many groups specialize in verse 11 of Jeremiah chapter 29: '"For I know the plans I have for you," declares the Lord, "plans to prosper you and not to harm you, plans to give you hope and a future."' Some people believe that God does not care about them when trouble comes their way. However, this is quite the opposite of what this verse means. Often, we cannot understand what God is doing. This verse is not intended to give you the idea that the Lord will keep you from ever being tested or from having a future that is easy. It is not a verse that suggests that you will not experience physical harm, sickness, relational troubles, employment layoffs, or any number of circumstances that may come against you in this life.

Rather, this verse speaks of spiritual blessings and plans of God that are greater than any physical blessing or future here on earth. It is a word that speaks of a hope and a future that the people of God (Christians) can have in Christ.

Don't attempt to force your plans or shortcut God's plan or timing. Throughout Scripture, God desires the redemption of all mankind. It is for the people of God to possess fellowship and eternal life with Him. God's plan for you is the same; to prosper and grow spiritually in Christ. His plan to offer you hope and a future has never changed. Your hope and future are in Jesus. God has made the mystery of salvation known to you, which He purposed in Christ. You have hope and a future in Jesus, a hope and future for eternal life with Him in glory. It is a hope and future that surpasses anything you know or understand. Do not put your hope in this life or what you can achieve with your hands. The situation you are in will not last forever. Look to the Lord, where your hope and help come from. Your future is in Christ, not in the doctors, the president, or the things of this world.

You have hope and a future in Christ. However, God does not intervene to stop you from making bad decisions or doing the wrong thing. At times, you may experience suffering due to someone else's sin, health problems, or natural disasters. But despite your mistakes or the difficulties that come your way, God has a purpose for your life. No matter what happens, God is in control, and He will continue to draw you back to His plan for your life.

IDENTIFYING GOD'S PLAN FOR OUR LIVES

I will consider this section regarding the question asked by Saul of Tarsus at the moment of his new birth: "What shall I do, Lord?" Did Saul's conversion just "happen" by chance on the Damascus road, or was it consistent with a divine plan and purpose? Acts 9:15 tells us that it was undoubtedly "according to plan" - God's plan. But does God have an idea for my life? If so, how can I know it and what is involved in finding it? These and many other questions demand a solution.

SOBER

1. The Lord features a definite plan and purpose for the lifetime of all of his children

There are three compelling reasons to believe this. Firstly, it is reasonable to expect it. If we are building a house or designing a dress, we work according to an idea or pattern. It is not unreasonable to think that God, being a God of order and method, would do the same.

Consider Abraham. By faith, when he was called to go out into a place that he would later receive as an inheritance, he obeyed and went out, not knowing where he was going. By faith, he sojourned in the land of promise as if he was in a foreign country, dwelling in tents with Isaac and Jacob, who were also heirs of the same promise. He did this because he was looking for a city with foundations, whose builder and maker is God (Hebrews 11:8-10).

Moses was a man of faith. When he came of age, he refused to be called the son of Pharaoh's daughter. Instead, he chose to suffer affliction with the people of God, rather than to enjoy the pleasures of sin for a season. He esteemed the reproach of Christ greater riches than the treasures in Egypt because he had respect for the recompense of the reward. By faith, Moses left Egypt without fearing the wrath of the king. He endured, as he could see him who is invisible. These verses from Hebrews 11:24-27 show us that Moses was a man who lived his life in faith, trusting in God even when facing difficult circumstances.

GOD'S PLAN

David (Now therefore thus shalt thou say unto my servant David, Thus saith the LORD of hosts, I took thee from the sheepcote, even from following the sheep, that thou shouldest be ruler over my people Israel. 1 Chronicles 17:7);

Isaiah (Also I heard the voice of the Lord, saying, Whom shall I send, and who will go for us? Then said I, Here am I; send me. Isaiah 6:8);

Jeremiah 1:5-8 says, "Before I formed you in the womb, I knew you; before you were born, I sanctified you and ordained you a prophet to the nations." Then I said, "Ah, Lord GOD! I cannot speak; I am only a child." But the LORD said to me, "Do not say, 'I am only a child.' For you will go to all whom I send you, and whatever I command you, you will speak. Do not be afraid of them, for I am with you to deliver you," says the LORD.

Paul (But the Lord said unto him, Go thy way: for he is a chosen vessel unto me, to bear my name before the Gentiles, and kings, and the children of Israel Acts 9:15). God's Word teaches it. search Ephesians 2:10, and compare Psalm 27:11; 37:23; 73:24; 148:8; Proverbs 3:6; 15:19; 16:3; Isaiah 6:8-9; 30:21 and James 1:5.

Notice the three subsequent characteristics of God's plan for our lives. It is a private plan, as evidenced by the use of the pronouns "you" and "me" in Acts 9:4. There is no one else in the world like you, and thus God's plan for you is unique and personal - meant for you alone! He has a purpose to fulfill in and through your life that cannot be fulfilled in or through the life of any other person. It is an ideal plan, as stated in Romans 12:2 (which should be read in conjunction with Romans 12:1). God's desire or plan for His children's lives is described as "his good, pleasing and perfect will." It is also a practical plan, as it is workable and it's thoroughly associated with everyday living and repair. It's not an idea which only sounds "good, pleasing and perfect" during a theoretical sense, but it proves to be so in experience!

2. **The foremost important thing in life, therefore, is to get God's plan and purpose for our life**

It's apparent, yet sadly true, that some Christians fail to grasp God's plan and purpose for their lives. As a result, their lives are filled with disappointment, defeat, frustration, and failure. How wonderful it is to feel that we are achieving something truly worthwhile and to understand that we do it not for ourselves but in accordance with the desire of our loving heavenly Father! Every unconverted person lives a self-planned life, just as Saul did before his conversion (see Acts 9:5). However, it's also unfortunately true that many Christians plan their own lives. We make decisions and choices that later prove to be wrong (compare John 21:3). There's nothing greater or more comforting than to know that we are in the center of God's will, and each one of us can know just that.

3. We enter God's plan once we accept and acknowledge Jesus as our Lord and Saviour

Saul entered into the plan of God when he submitted to what the Lord told him to do, as recorded in Acts 9:6. In verse 8, we see that the Lord Jesus revealed Himself to Saul, saying, "I am Jesus...that is, 'Savior'" (see Matthew 1:21). This is not to say that God was not interested in Saul and watching over him before his conversion, but it is true to say that Saul only truly entered into the plan of God when he bowed at the feet of Jesus and accepted Him as his Savior and Lord.

4. We continue to get as we continue in God's plan, by a daily submission to him and to his revealed will

He has the entire plan of our lives ahead of Him, but He only reveals it to us bit by bit. (See Psalm 37:23.) God knows the beginning from the end (Isaiah 46:9-10). However, to understand and try to do God's will, we must meet a human condition, which is complete submission to Him and a strong desire to obey Him. (See Acts 22:10.) This inquiry into God's will involves four things:

- Communion with Him in prayer. An appropriate prayer is recorded in Psalm 27:11. It's when we make a habit of regularly going into the secret place that the Lord graciously reveals His plan to us, step by step.
- Studying and searching His Word, how wonderfully all the saints of God are led as they read and submit their lives to the commands and guidance of the Word of God! Search Psalm 119:105.

- Prompt and unquestioning obedience is crucial. God reveals His will as we obey Him – see I Samuel 15:22. He only reveals it one step at a time; for example, Saul had to travel into the town before the Lord told him the subsequent step He wanted him to take (Acts 9:6).

- Complete and implicit trust is required because we will rarely perceive God's workings in our lives. We live by faith and not by sight, which means we have to trust Him. The Lord chose Saul to be "a chosen instrument," and Saul had to trust God in everything He permitted in his life—sufferings, privations, stoning, imprisonments, and more (2 Corinthians 11:24-28). We must remember that God's plan includes His permission of life's testing. This is evident in 1 Peter 4:12-13 and 19.

CHAPTER THREE

GOD'S INTENTION

How can we understand God's intentions for us? This is an important factor that can help us grasp the situations of our lives and improve upon them. 3 John 2 says, "Beloved, I wish above all things that thou mayest prosper and be in health, even as thy soul prospereth.

God's intentions for our lives are comprehensive and cover all facets of life. As per the above verse, it is clear that the details of His intentions include physical prosperity in all forms, health prosperity in all forms, and soul prosperity. God's plan for our lives encompasses our finances, jobs, accommodation, and other aspects that contribute to a good life. Health is also inclusive, which includes having perfect mental and physical health. Having good mental health does not involve being constantly addicted to stimulants. Lastly, our soul prosperity is based on our salvation, Christian living, and hope of a blissful destiny with God. I will divide this section based on the three parts of the verse.

BELOVED, I WISH IN ALL THINGS THAT THOU MAYEST PROSPER

This indicates that God intends for us to achieve success in all temporal affairs and in all aspects of our lives.

SOBER

Since such success depends on the blessings of God, who makes us rich, it is important to pray and ask for His blessings.

The Bible is considered the greatest book in the world when it comes to money management, leading to staggering prosperity. Throughout history, God's children have been prosperous. For instance, in the book of Genesis, we learn that Abraham was rich in cattle, silver, and gold. Solomon, known as the richest man in the world, would have been a trillionaire by today's standards. His horse stables were even made of gold. That's true prosperity! Jesus gave us 38 parables, 16 of which focus on how to manage our possessions. The New Testament contains over 500 verses about prayer and less than 500 about faith. In contrast, there are more than 2,000 verses instructing us on how to manage our possessions to attain prosperity in our lives. It's crucial to understand that if you don't master your money, it will end up mastering you. The choice is entirely yours.

You will never prosper until you believe that it is God's will for you to prosper. The difference between a life of prosperity and a life of want is choice. Your financial success tomorrow will be determined by your obedience to God's Word today. If you plant a seed this afternoon, it will not grow into a stalk of corn by tomorrow morning. Today, you have the choice to honor God with your living and giving, so that He can open the windows of heaven and bless you.

GOD'S INTENTION

Whenever God gives you the opportunity to give, He is also giving you the chance to increase your income. Let go of what's in your hand so that God can bless you with what He holds in His. What He has planned for you is far greater than what you can achieve on your own. He owns all the wealth in the world, and your income is determined by your obedience to His Word.

I want you to understand the principle of seed time and harvest. Everything that God does on Earth is based on this fundamental principle. A student who studies hard is expected to do well in their exams. A business person who wakes up early and follows ethical business practices is expected to make a profit. A farmer who sows seeds is expected to reap the produce at a later time. These are the principles that work.

Everything that God controls... GIVES! The sun gives light, clouds give rain, and God gave his only Son so that we could be redeemed. What are you giving? You must offer to God what's in your hand, so that you can reap what you sow. Even unbelievers know the power of investment. If you've ever read Robert Kiyosaki's books, you'll understand that investment is the act of sowing the seeds that we have in our hand. Acquiring luxurious materials and assets may increase our expenses without yielding profits for us. God wants us to prosper, but we must understand the principle of prosperity, which lies in giving. Only an open hand can receive.

SOBER

There's a story about a wealthy Texan who wanted to be buried in his beloved Cadillac. When he passed away, the undertakers dug a large grave and used a lowering device to place the car inside. They dressed the deceased in his finest sportswear, placed a cigar in his mouth, and positioned him behind the wheel with the speedometer set to 80 miles per hour.

The mourners gathered around the grave as the unusual coffin slowly sank into the ground. With the acceptable words of committal, a millionaire friend of the deceased brushed a tear from his eye and sighed, "Man, that's living!" He said it with boldness and pride.

But, of course, it's not living - it's death! That is the reality of it, no matter how glamorous the burial may seem with a Cadillac grave. A dead man is a dead man, and true prosperity cannot be measured by material possessions or even by being a millionaire. True prosperity lies in being rich with God. God desires that we be prosperous, but we must acquire our riches with His principles. We need not envy those who ride in Cadillacs or cruise the streets with flashy, luxurious properties. There is still hope for the living. As long as we are alive, there will always be a tomorrow.

AND BE IN HEALTH;

The health of the body is the most desirable of all outward mercies because without it, the richest delicacies, the most important possessions, or the dearest friends are of little value. Without good health, one cannot fully enjoy any of these blessings. Therefore, good health is the primary and most important outward mercy that one can wish for and desire for oneself and others. The rule and measure of this wish should be in accordance with the prosperity of one's soul.

Matthew Henry's concise commentary suggests that those who are in Christ should love their brothers for his sake. Grace and health are great companions, as grace can use health to fulfill its purpose. Even if the body is weak, a rich soul can be lodged in it, and in that case, grace must be exercised. There is a parallel between the spiritual and natural aspects of a person.

Exercise is a key component of maintaining good health. It involves physical activity specifically designed to sustain or improve fitness. Our bodies were not designed to be idle but rather to be in motion. As the temple that houses the presence of God, we must keep our bodies active and healthy. Sometimes, we abuse this temple by consuming things that do not benefit our health.

If God intends for our bodies to be healthy, then we must be mindful of how we treat our bodies. Otherwise, we may end up working against God's intentions for our lives. Drinking alcohol and using other stimulants does not align with God's intentions. It is no wonder that sobriety is mentioned several times in the scriptures.

Exercise involves more than just physical movement. To achieve ultimate results and maintain a healthy and balanced life, one must exercise the mind, body, and soul. Exercise should also be accompanied by healthy eating habits. Often, the reason for our poor health is due to consuming unhealthy junk food. It is crucial to have proper nutrition, which involves providing or obtaining the necessary food for health and growth. It is understandable why the scripture is so descriptive in its context, as it wishes for us to prosper in health just as our soul prospers. Our overall health depends on what we put into our bodies.

Thomas Fuller once said, "Health is not valued till sickness comes." Therefore, we must realize the value of life and cherish every moment. Taking care of the vessel that God has loaned us for the time we have on this earth is crucial. If we take care of our bodies, they will take care of us. Here are a few tips to become a well-rounded and healthy individual:

Maintain a daily exercise routine

No, you do not need to force yourself into intense workouts at the gym, but you should aim to stay as active as possible. You can stick to simple floor exercises, swimming, walking, or simply keep yourself moving by performing some household chores. Do what your body allows you to do.

What is important and essential is that you continue exercising. Dedicate at least twenty to thirty minutes every day for exercise, and aim to exercise a minimum of three to five times a week. Make it a habit to incorporate enough physical activity into your daily routine.

Be conscious in your diet

To maintain a healthy lifestyle, it is important to eat a healthy diet. Incorporate more fruits and vegetables into your meals and reduce your intake of carbohydrates, high sodium, and unhealthy fats. Avoid consuming processed foods and sweets. Skipping meals should be avoided as it can increase your body's urge to eat more when you resume eating. Remember to burn more calories than you consume.

Engage in the activities that you are passionate about. Occasionally, take a break from the stress and demands of life and do something that you enjoy doing.

Surround yourself with positive energy

To maintain a sound mental and emotional state, it is important to surround yourself with positive energy. While it may not always be possible to avoid problems, it is helpful to approach obstacles with an optimistic outlook. Surround yourself with supportive friends and individuals who can offer constructive criticism to help you improve.

Make it a habit to always check out the brighter side of life. albeit you discover yourself within the worst situation, there's always an upside to it—something good and positive. Linger over this stuff instead.

SOBER

Maintaining a healthy lifestyle isn't that difficult, nor does it require tons of labor. Just keep doing what you are doing and apply the staying healthy tips listed above—surely you'll be a well-rounded individual in no time.

EVEN AS THY SOUL PROSPERETH:

How exactly does the soul prosper? The soul is diseased with sin and can only be considered healthy when all its iniquities are forgiven. The soul prospers when it has a spiritual craving for the Gospel, feeds on the sincere milk of the Word, is nourished by it, and grows through it. It prospers when it is actively engaged in practicing religion, hope, and love, and when its spiritual knowledge is increasing. It prospers when it grows in grace and knowledge of Christ Jesus, and when its inward strength is renewed daily. It prospers when it enjoys communion with God, experiences the sunshine of His countenance, and therefore the joys of His salvation. Finally, it prospers when it is fruitful in every good work.

If you want to undergo transformation, you need to change the way you think. This will lead to a change in your life as well. To understand God's will, we need to renew our minds by exchanging our beliefs (which are often influenced by the world) for God's beliefs. Remember that it is not you who transforms yourself, but rather God who does the transforming. You should allow Him to work on you by letting everything that enters your heart pass through the filter of His Word. You will know that you have been changed when you begin to speak and react differently to things. When you change your mind, your heart will follow suit.

Renewing your mind allows God's Word to enter into your life. As a believer, you have the Holy Spirit living within you. Change is inevitable, but through the power of God's Word, you can renew your mind and become a new person. The question is, how are you renewing your mind? Are you focusing on the Word or the world? Remember, garbage in, garbage out. If you don't like the results you are getting, you need to change the seed that you are planting in your mind.

Another effective way to bring the soul into prosperity mode is to rejoice in God. Our lives reflect what we focus on. If the image we see of ourselves is from this world, then we will manifest what this world has to offer. This includes negative emotions such as anger, confusion, fear, pain, sickness, lack...

When we examine God's Word, we see a reflection of Christ. That is who you truly are. After you put the Word down, do you still envision yourself as Christ in your mind, or do you revert back to the world's perception of yourself? The thoughts we hold about ourselves will manifest in our lives. Do you love yourself? Do you expect blessings to come your way? God does. He sees you as Christ.

When we have a lower view of ourselves than what God declares about us, we are essentially passing judgment on ourselves. We tend to punish ourselves for not being flawless and start expecting people to treat us accordingly, thus creating a self-fulfilling prophecy. This negative mindset distorts our perception of everything. Instead, we must let go of these beliefs and choose to see ourselves as God sees us. When we surrender these thoughts to Him, He removes them from our hearts. If you sense a burden or heaviness in your heart, it's a clear sign of such judgment. Financial blessings and good health come from God and not solely from the physical realm. While we can activate God's principles regarding finances and health, they stem from a prosperous soul. As we align ourselves with God, blessings from heaven manifest in our lives.

Fear and doubt have no place in our lives. They hinder our ability to hear God's voice clearly. When our soul prospers, nothing can obstruct the blessings that come our way. Our external reality reflects what we're experiencing internally.

Everything we desire in life can be attributed to our souls thriving. In January, I set a goal for myself for the year: to live like Christ. I wrote down the steps I would take to achieve this. Now, I realize that living like Christ is a manifestation of my soul prospering, which is the only thing I need to focus on. If my soul is thriving, everything else will fall into place. When my soul is healed, it will have a positive impact on my physical, emotional, and mental well-being.

CHAPTER FOUR

THE HELMET OF SALVATION

"And take the helmet of salvation, and the sword of the Spirit,
which is the word of God" (Ephesians 6:17).

When Paul wrote to the Ephesians about the helmet of salvation, many of them may have recognized the analogy from the book of Isaiah. In Isaiah 59:17, God is described as wearing both the breastplate of righteousness and the helmet of salvation. By referencing this Old Testament scripture, Paul emphasizes that the armor of God is, in every sense, the same armor that God Himself wears. This also prompts us to consider what salvation is, what it means for us, and how it relates to a helmet. So, what was the purpose of a helmet in the Roman army? The Roman helmet, known as a "galea," protected the head from enemy attacks. Since mass production did not exist at that time, each helmet was individually made, resulting in varying designs. Typically, the helmets were made of metal, though poorer soldiers or those from earlier times in the empire may have worn leather helmets reinforced with metal pieces.

SOBER

The helmet's most obvious value was to protect against blows to the head. Helmets usually had cheek plates to safeguard the face and a metal piece at the back to shield the rear of the neck. Moreover, during the first century, helmets began to include a brow ridge to provide protection for the eyes. In warfare, the enemy often targeted the head since a soldier's mind controlled their decisions and reactions during a fight. Harming the head was advantageous in combat. Similarly, our enemy, Satan, does the same! When a soldier prepared for battle, the helmet was the last piece of armor to be put on. It represented the final act of readiness before combat. A helmet was essential for survival as it protected the brain, the command center for the rest of the body. If the head was severely damaged, the rest of the armor would be of little use.

The assurance of salvation is our impenetrable defense against anything the enemy throws at us. Jesus said, "Do not be afraid of those who kill the body but cannot kill the soul. Rather, be afraid of the One who can destroy both soul and body in hell" (Matthew 10:28). The idea in this verse is that, as we prepare for Satan's attacks, we must grab that helmet and buckle it on tightly. But what is salvation? Salvation means being saved—receiving deliverance. For Christians, salvation means receiving freedom from the penalty of sin. It means "to be rescued, delivered." And we can be delivered or rescued from almost anything negative. Whenever you see the words "salvation" or "saved" in the Bible, you should pause, substitute in the word "deliverance" or "delivered"... and then look within the context to understand what kind of deliverance is being talked about. When you do that, you'll see that salvation in the Bible is deliverance from enemies, sickness, premature death, the devastating consequences of sin in our lives, and a wide variety of other calamities.

The helmet of salvation is a mindset. Salvation is not limited to a one-time act of the past or a future hope. God's salvation is an ongoing, eternal state that His children enjoy in the present. It provides daily protection and deliverance from our sin nature and Satan's schemes. Thanks to the power of the cross, our enemy no longer has any hold on us. He knows that, but he also knows that most of God's children do not know that—or, at least, they do not live as if they know. We must learn to keep our helmets buckled so that his fiery missiles do not occupy our thoughts and set us ablaze (2 Corinthians 10:5).

There are several actions a believer can fancy keep this Helmet of Salvation fastened and functioning:

1. Renew our minds. Our minds are battlefields. The outcomes of these battles determine the course of our lives. Romans 12:1–2 instructs us to renew our minds by allowing the reality of God's Word to wipe out anything contrary thereto. Old ideas, opinions, and worldviews must be replaced. We must permit God's truth to repeatedly wash away the world's filth, lies, and confusion from our minds and adopt God's perspective.

2. Reject doubts that arise from circumstances. We, as human beings, are sensory creatures. What we cannot comprehend with our five senses, we tend to disregard. If we allow them to, circumstances may convince us that God doesn't truly love us or that His Word isn't true. It's impossible to have faith and doubt at the same time. God rewards our faith. With the helmet of salvation firmly in place, we can choose to believe what appears impossible (Hebrews 11:6; 1 Peter 1:8–9).

3. Keep an endless perspective. When life crashes in on us, we must remember to "look up." Our salvation is the most precious gift we have received. Keeping our eyes on it can help us weather life's storms. We can choose to live our lives by the motto: "If it doesn't have eternal significance, it's not important."

4. Remember that victory is already accomplished. When we consider ourselves "dead to sin but alive to God" (Romans 6:11), we eliminate many of the opportunities Satan uses to entrap us. When choosing sin is no longer an option for us because we recognize ourselves as "new creatures", we effectively stop many avenues of failure.

5. Find the entirety of our hope in Him. Psalm 73:25 says, "Whom have I in heaven but You? Besides You, I desire nothing on earth." Our helmet is best when we treasure what it represents. The salvation Jesus bought for us cannot share the place of importance in our hearts with earthly things. When pleasing the Lord is our highest

delight, we eliminate many of Satan's lures and render his evil suggestions powerless.

As we wear the helmet of salvation every day, our minds become more insulated against the suggestions, desires, and traps the enemy lays for us. We choose to protect our minds from excessive worldly influence and instead think on things that honor Christ (Philippians 4:8). In doing so, we put on our salvation as a protective helmet that can "guard our hearts and minds in Christ Jesus" (Philippians 4:7; compare with Isaiah 26:3 and 1 Peter 1:5).

THE HELMET FOR THE CHRISTIAN

First and foremost, like all other pieces of armor, it is important to recognize that the helmet of salvation is also a gift from God and belongs to Him. Isaiah 59:17 depicts God donning the helmet of salvation when He battles against wickedness, so this helmet is not our own salvation, but rather a gift from God that we receive when we believe in Jesus for eternal life. The helmet of salvation is God's helmet that He has bestowed upon us for our use as soldiers in the war against spiritual forces.

But what exactly is this helmet? In verse 17, Isaiah tells us that the helmet is salvation. Similarly, in Ephesians, when Paul speaks of salvation, he is referring to various aspects of our deliverance from the penalty of sin, specifically justification. Therefore, we should understand the helmet of salvation in Ephesians 6:17 as the helmet of justification salvation that we are called to take up and wear.

Why does this matter for Christians, especially in spiritual warfare? What use is the helmet of salvation for Christian soldiers in battle? It cannot mean they need to be saved since God only gives His armor to those who are already saved. You don't become saved by putting on the helmet. If you have the helmet to put on, you're already saved. So how does the helmet help Christians in spiritual battle? Well, the helmet protects the head, and more specifically, the brain which contains knowledge about salvation. Satan often attacks what a Christian does or doesn't know, and regarding the helmet of salvation, Paul tells us that one of the truths Satan tries to attack is whether we have salvation or not. Simply put, wearing the helmet gives us the reassurance of salvation. Assurance of salvation is ultimately a matter of the mind, knowledge, and faith in God. All knowledge is contained within the mind.

The knowledge of what Christ has done for us is contained in our brains. We made the choice to believe in Jesus for eternal life, and we know what we have in Christ, including our salvation. So, when Paul says to take up the helmet of salvation, he means to remember, know, and understand in our minds that we are saved, justified, and secure in Jesus' arms. Wearing the helmet of salvation means having the knowledge and understanding of the reassurance of our salvation. Later, I'll discuss how to have assurance of salvation when we talk about putting on the helmet. But before that, I want to address a misconception about assurance.

Some people seem to believe that the reassurance of salvation and the associated eternal security can be interpreted as a license to indulge in sin. They may think, "Well, since I am saved and secure, and I can never lose my salvation, I can go ahead and live however I want, just like the devil." Theoretically, logically, and biblically speaking, a Christian could technically do that. It is true that if you are saved, and you choose to live a life of sin, you cannot lose your salvation. You will still go to heaven. However, Christians should not adopt this mindset, and in fact, most Christians do not. There are several reasons why Christians should not take this approach, and one of them relates to what we are currently discussing.

The helmet on a soldier's armor was never intended to be the primary line of defense against the enemy. Similarly, in spiritual warfare, the helmet of salvation, which represents the knowledge and assurance that one is saved, is not the only line of defense. In spiritual battle, one should not say, "Well, I'm saved and secure forever, so I can lower my defenses, put down my shield, live however I want, and let the enemy attack me because 'Hey, I've got my helmet on.'" A soldier who does this will end up receiving many blows to the head. Even though the soldier may survive because of the helmet, they will not be much use in battle and may soon lose their hearing, sight, ability to think, and possibly suffer serious brain damage or premature death. A Christian who takes too many blows to the helmet of salvation does not lose their salvation, but they may end up like Mohammed Ali, the great boxer who took too many blows to the head and now can barely remember who he is and what he has done in the past. It is a tragic thing when a Christian wastes or abuses the wonderful and gracious gift of assurance as an excuse for sin. They end up as decapitated Christians, the living dead, walking around forgetful of who they are and what they should be doing, or what God has done for them in Christ. It is indeed very sad.

You see, the helmet is the last line of defense, not the primary. The shield of faith and the breastplate of righteousness are the pieces of armor that are meant to take most of the blows. The helmet is merely there for the attacks that get past these. If you're living virtuously by walking in faith, but suddenly find yourself in sin, and Satan has, through his wily schemes, managed to get one of his flaming darts in, and he comes in and starts to taunt you - "Oh, a Christian wouldn't do this. Are you sure you're a Christian?" "Oh, a Christian wouldn't have said that word. Maybe you're not a Christian after all." "You skipped your devotions today? Perhaps you've lost your salvation." - Bring out the last line of defense - the helmet of salvation. Satan has breached the shield of faith and the breastplate of righteousness and is now attacking your salvation. He's challenging you to question

THE HELMET OF SALVATION

whether you were ever saved or not, and making you doubt whether you're truly a Christian. At times, he may even try to make you believe that you've lost your salvation.

That God may not love you anymore. That God has given up on you. That God has folded His arms and turned His back on you." These are deceptions that Satan tells you. Ultimately, all of those are blows to the helmet of salvation, and they hurt. I have been in this situation before, and it feels like you've stuck your head in an iron bucket and then someone whacked the outside with a sledgehammer. WHAM! Your spiritual ears are ringing, your mind is spinning, and you can't see straight. Worry and doubt creep in, and panic sets in. It's not a good feeling to have the helmet of salvation take a blow from the enemy. But guess what? You had your helmet on. Yes, you have that ringing in your ears and the stars swirling around your head, but at least it's not your brains all over the sidewalk. And in these situations, if you have your helmet on, if you know what the Bible says about your salvation in Jesus, you can be sure that you are saved, no matter what lies the devil throws your way. You may have seen the T-shirt that says, "When the devil reminds you of your past, remind him of his future." That's what the helmet of salvation does for the Christian. It provides you with the reassurance of salvation. And it should be the last line of defense, not the first. So when you sin, as we all still do, you can say, "Yes, I've sinned, but thanks be to God, through Jesus our Lord, I'm still saved!

SOBER

Before discussing how to take up the helmet, let me address another important issue. In today's world, the question of eternal security and the assurance of salvation is often seen as a divisive topic. Some churches and Christians avoid discussing it to maintain unity within the church. While I understand the reasoning behind this approach, I believe that if we lose or sidestep the truths of eternal security and assurance of salvation, we risk losing a significant part of the gospel. In fact, we risk losing the battle for the truth of the Gospel altogether. If God is not able to keep us saved once we are saved, then how can we trust that He can save us in the first place? If God is not able to save us once we are secured and sealed, how can we believe that He is able to save us when we are depraved, lost, and dead in trespasses and sins? Furthermore, if we believe that we need works to maintain our salvation or to prove that we are saved, then it's not a stretch to say that we also need works to get saved. Unfortunately, many churches are headed in this direction, and when we do, the Gospel begins to crumble.

Do you want to understand one of the indications that historians say signaled the start of the Roman Empire's downfall? Believe it or not, some historians suggest that the beginning of the end for the Roman Empire was when soldiers stopped wearing helmets. In his book, "The Rise and Fall of the Roman Empire," Gibbon notes that the relaxation of discipline and the disuse of exercise made soldiers unable to withstand the fatigue of service. They complained about the

THE HELMET OF SALVATION

weight of their armor and eventually received permission to discard some of it, including the helmet. The Church, on the other hand, cannot afford to discard any pieces of the armor, including the helmet. Although this has caused some division within the Church, and some may want to ignore or sidestep it, this is only because some soldiers have become undisciplined, stopped exercising, and lost their fitness.

The assurance of salvation as given here but the helmet isn't something we will afford to get aside. Rather, Paul says in verse 17, we are to put it on.

PUTTING ON THE HELMET

So let me conclude by teaching you ways to require up the helmet of salvation. The way to know that you simply are saved. The way to know that you simply are safe and secure forever.

First and foremost, as indicated by this particular piece of armor, the assurance of salvation is based on knowledge rather than works. It depends on what and Who you know, rather than what you have or have not done. Allow me to demonstrate this through a few Scripture passages that affirm the concept of eternal security and, consequently, the reassurance of salvation.

The Gospel of John is an excellent resource on the topic of the assurance of salvation. Repeatedly, we encounter verses that state that anyone who solely believes in Jesus for eternal life will receive it.

SOBER

Romans 8:31-39 is a classic passage regarding the security of the believer. In this section, we learn that once we are saved and justified by God, nothing can separate us from His love. This includes anything in heaven or on earth, including angels or demons, and even ourselves. Therefore, nothing we do can sever our connection to God's love.

Another passage that has helped many people gain assurance is 1 John 5:11-13. I prefer to require people through this passage, asking them a couple of simple questions on the text. These questions are as follow:

What has God given us?

Where is that in this life?

Who has eternal life?

How do they get eternal life?

Who doesn't have eternal life?

Is there any alternative?

Has this been written in order that we may hope we've eternal life?

Is God making a promise?

Would God mislead us?

Have you received the Son?

Then does one know that you simply have eternal life?

On what ground or basis are you able to know this?

When are you able to know this?

THE HELMET OF SALVATION

The assurance of salvation holds great importance in living the Christian life in a proper manner. While some may view it as a peripheral or controversial doctrine, I believe it is central. Knowing that God loves us unconditionally, regardless of how much or how often we may stumble, brings us immense peace and comfort in our Christian journey. This unconditional and infinite love serves as a powerful motivator to help us strive towards living a Christ-like life.

One of my favorite theologians may be a musician by the name of Steve Taylor. In one of his songs, he writes, "People think better when they don't have a gun at their head." And that's true of Christians as well. Christians are better able to live out their faith when they don't have to constantly worry about whether or not they are saved. If we go around constantly wondering or hoping that we're saved, we're not going to be very effective in our Christian walk. But if we know that we're going to heaven, regardless of what happens, that frees us up to focus on other things and to fully engage in the task at hand.

Did you know that when construction began on the Golden Gate Bridge in San Francisco, progress was initially slow for quite some time? It wasn't due to a shortage of workers or funding; they had plenty of both. The reason was that the workers were afraid to work over the cold, icy waters of the San Francisco Bay. They worked slowly out of fear of falling to their deaths. Sadly, twelve men did fall to their deaths, which made the remaining workers even more fearful and caused them to work even more slowly. As a result, each passing day brought further delays in the project's completion.

Eventually, the contractor had the idea to install a safety net below the bridge. It ran from one side of the bay to the other, underneath the workers, so that if they fell, they would be caught by the net and remain safe. As a result, the work progressed much more quickly. Although two men did fall from the bridge, neither of them died. The presence of the safety net provided the workers with a sense of security, allowing them to focus solely on their work and not worry about maintaining their balance in the windy conditions of the San Francisco Bay. Ultimately, the bridge was completed on time, and the safety net played a significant role in achieving this goal.

Have you been feeling tempted by the devil to give up? Has he been telling you that you cannot be a true Christian and that God no longer loves you? Do not believe these lies. Put on the helmet of salvation and remember the comforting and reassuring teachings of the Word of God. Remember that there is a safety net beneath you if you fall, and that net is the loving hand of God. The Bible tells us in John 10:27-29: "My sheep hear my voice, and I know them, and they follow me. And I give them eternal life, and they shall never perish, neither shall anyone snatch them out of my hand. My Father, who has given them to me, is greater than all, and no one is able to snatch them out of my Father's hand."

THE HELMET OF SALVATION

Despite our continued sins, God loves us. He will not take us out of His protective hand, and neither can anyone else, not even Satan. Do not allow Satan's lies to enter your mind. Put on the helmet of salvation and remember that if you have believed in Jesus for eternal life, you are safe and secure forever.

CHAPTER FIVE

THE BRAIN PUZZLES

Jacqueline Woodson once said, "Diversity is about all of us, and about us having to figure out how to walk through this world together." It is important to recognize that people can never be equal in capacity, but there is greater strength in diversity than in uniformity. This strength is identified when we properly perceive the nuances behind the diverse things we see. I believe that our diversity makes us stronger, smarter, and more innovative, which helps us better serve the needs of our people and community. However, if we do not solve and manage the puzzles of diversity, it could lead to misunderstanding, battles of the mind, rancor, and even affect the mental state of individuals and processes. As Paul said in 1 Corinthians 12:4, "Now there are diversities of gifts, but the same Spirit."

Although Paul does not explicitly state it, there is little doubt that during his 18 months in Corinth, he taught the saints about spiritual gifts. Such knowledge was crucial for building up the body by the Spirit as He worked through each believer's specific gifts. However, it is clear that they had largely forgotten these vital truths, which resulted in much perversion and confusion.

The point is that diversity within the church comes from the same divine source. Consequently, conformity is not necessary for unity. What is necessary for unity is the Lordship of Jesus. The Corinthian Christians were behaving in response to the flesh instead of the Spirit. They quarreled, became factious, took one another to court, fell back into immoral and idolatrous practices, corrupted marriage relationships, abused their Christian liberty, and became self-centered, overconfident, and worldly. Their misunderstanding and misuse of spiritual gifts were serious results of their carnal divisiveness.

In 1 Corinthians 12:4, Paul wrote, "Now there are varieties of gifts, but the same Spirit - the same Spirit is the source of all of them." Paul used the term "pneumatikos" for Spiritual (gifts) and, at this time, uses a synonym for gifts ("charismata" - meaning "gift of grace" or "free gift"). "Pneumatikos" emphasizes the Spirit as the source, and "charismata" emphasizes that the gifts are the result of grace, not merit or earning. The gifts are representative of the divine enablement of believers to minister in the power of the Holy Spirit and for the glory of God. "Varieties" is a term of contrast that highlights the different gifts but unified Source (and the same purpose - edification). So, while there is diversity, there is also unity because all gifts are from the same Spirit, who energizes unity (Ephesians 4:3) and enables the edification of the Body, as Paul said to the Ephesians, "There is one body and one Spirit" (Ephesians 4:4). In other words, what Paul is emphasizing here with the word "varieties" (also used in the next two verses) is that there is variety and diversity within the gifts, ministries, and effects, but there is only one source, the Holy Spirit, and one purpose, edification. While the Corinthians considered the more "spectacular gifts" as more important, Paul is making it clear from the outset that they are all important, for all of them originate from the same Holy Spirit, and all are necessary for edification.

Peter provides a summary of the two general types of spiritual gifts, namely speaking and serving gifts. As everyone has received a unique gift, they should use it to serve others as good stewards. It's important to note that these gifts are not for personal gain, and we will be held accountable for our use of them. The purpose of these gifts is to serve others and demonstrate the manifold grace of God. Those who speak should speak as if they are speaking the very words of God, while those who serve should do so with the strength that God provides. Ultimately, our goal should be to glorify God through Jesus, to whom belongs all glory and dominion forever and ever. Amen. (1 Peter 4:10-11+)

As we contemplate on how God created and distributed gifts through the same Spirit, we may be puzzled by the necessity for these differences in gifts. Each gift may manifest in a unique way, distinct from others. It is important to approach this puzzle with a sober mind and strive to understand these differences, just as the Corinthian church did. When we face challenges in life that affect our thoughts and emotions, we need to work on deciphering the puzzle and recognize that differences are inevitable. Only a mature mind can truly comprehend the significance of these puzzles. We should learn to appreciate the diversity in life and operate according to our own gifts, in order to be mentally effective and mature in our mindset.

RIGHT PERCEPTION OF THE MIND

Kurt, Liane, and Adam state in their article, titled "Mind Perception is the Essence of Morality," that "mind perception entails ascribing mental capacities to other entities, whereas moral judgment entails labeling entities as good or bad or actions as right or wrong." Additionally, the scripture defends our capacity as asserted by Apostle Paul to Timothy, stating, "For God hath not given us the spirit of fear; but of power, and of love, and of a sound mind" (KJV) (2 Timothy 1:7).

Have you ever felt like you were losing your mind due to the pressures, fears, exhaustion, and temptations of life? According to this passage, you are not losing your mind. God promises that you have been given a sound mind. God does not give the spirit of fear; instead, he gives a spirit of power, love, and a sound mind. The promise of a sound mind works even in difficult times. The word "sound" used in this context means a disciplined and self-controlled mind, as well as a mind that is saved, delivered from sin, revived, and protected. The word's meaning also encompasses your framework of thinking, your rationale, and your logic. The truth behind this verse is that God has given you a mind that is protected. When you abide in God's word, it protects your emotions and attitudes and safeguards you from the devil's assaults. It is essential for you to understand this text because it helps you live a life of faith, which is God's delight and enables you to do what God has asked you to do. Do not allow the devil to mess with your mentality or emotions or stop you from achieving your goals. Instead, rely on God's promise of a sound mind and let his word guide your thoughts and actions. Trust in God's protection and know that he will always be with you, even in difficult times.

An intense battle is raging around us twenty-four hours a day. In 1965, Donald Grey Barnhouse wrote a book called "The Invisible War," which described this war as the vicious battle for your mind. It is extreme, inexorable, and unfair because Satan never plays fair. The reason it is so intense is that your greatest asset is your mind. When the devil tries to convince you that you are losing your mind, remind him of 2 Timothy 1:7. Show him the promise of God's Word, and he will flee.

To protect your mind from the devil's attacks, focus on Jesus and declare daily that your mind is guarded by God's promises. By doing this, you will never go astray, as the Bible states, "For God hath not given us the spirit of fear, but of power, and of love, and of a sound mind."

DESTROYING STRONGHOLDS

I have seen the face of mental illness. I have witnessed firsthand what it's like when people are unable to hear God's voice because their minds are broken and cannot seem to connect with Him, even when they desire to do so. I know that anything that captures our minds, captivates us. Therefore, one of the most crucial things we need to learn and teach others is how to protect, strengthen, and renew our minds because the battle against sin always begins in the mind.

There are a lot of passages in Scripture that we could look at in this chapter, but I want us to focus on one: 2 Corinthians 10:3-5. It reads, "For though we walk in the flesh, we do not war according to the flesh, for the weapons of our warfare are not of the flesh, but divinely powerful for the destruction of fortresses. We are destroying speculations and every lofty thing raised up against the knowledge of God, and we are taking every thought captive to the obedience of Christ." Paul is telling us that our job during this battle is to "destroy strongholds." Do you recognize what a stronghold is? It's a barrier. Paul is talking about arguments and pretensions that are set up against the knowledge of God. This is a mental battle. And he says, "Destroy these strongholds." A stronghold can be one of two things:

It is often a worldview, such as materialism, hedonism, Darwinism, secularism, relativism, or communism that can become a mental stronghold. These "-isms" are mental forces that people create in opposition to the knowledge of God,

A stronghold can also refer to a personal attitude. Worries, seeking the approval of others, or anything that becomes an idol in your life can become strongholds. Fear, guilt, resentment, and insecurity are all examples of strongholds that can exist in your mind. The Bible teaches us to tear down these strongholds.

BRINGING EVERY THOUGHT CAPTIVE

Let's examine the last expression in the passage: "bringing into captivity every thought to the obedience of Christ." The original Greek word used in this passage, aichmaløtizø, means "to control, to conquer, to bring into submission." We are meant to suppress, control, and remand thoughts that are not obedient to Christ and make them obedient instead. Hupakøe is interpreted as "to bring into submission, to bring under control." The question that arises is how to achieve this feat of making our minds ours and teaching others to do the same. How do we bring our minds under control? Often, our minds are disobedient, disloyal, and defiant. They are driven by our wants and desires, and they may stray from our intended path. When we try to focus on something, our thoughts tend to wander, and when we want to pray, our thoughts may float away.

Paul discusses this topic in Romans 7, where he says, "For the good that I would, I do not: but the evil which I would not, that I do. . . . O wretched man that I am! Who shall deliver me from the body of this death?" (Romans 7:19, 24). The truth is that many Christians today are ineffective because they don't know how to fight the battle of the mind. It's crucial to make a concerted effort to understand how to overcome this battle.

CHAPTER SIX

RENEWING YOUR MIND

The mind is a powerful entity within us. With a controlled mind, we can achieve any feat in life - whether it's in business, academics, a happy family life, or a stress-free lifestyle. There is a common saying that goes, "Your mind is a garden, and your thoughts are the seeds. You can grow flowers or you can grow weeds." Buddy Owens also said, "When you fix your thoughts on God, God fixes your thoughts." The scripture also supports the need to renew our mind, as Apostle Paul said, "And we have received God's Spirit (not the world's spirit) so that we can know the wonderful things God has freely given us... But we understand these things, for we have the mind of Christ" (1 Corinthians 2:12, 16 NLT).

The Holy Spirit dwells within every believer to assist them in the process of renewing their minds. Having the mind of Christ refers to the ongoing process of the Holy Spirit revealing the thoughts and plans of God to our hearts and minds. Jesus taught that the Holy Spirit would be our Helper, and one of the primary ways He helps us is by revealing the mind or thinking of Christ to us.

"When the Spirit of Truth comes, He will guide you into all truth. He will not speak on His own, but will tell you what He has heard. He will also tell you about the future and bring Me glory by revealing to you whatever He receives from Me." (John 16:13 NLT)

Each believer can rely on the inner presence of the Holy Ghost to guide them, as He lives inside us to inform us of what Jesus and the Father want us to understand. The primary way He speaks to us is through the Scriptures, and we can ask Him to help us understand God and His Word. As the psalmist wrote, "Open my eyes, that I may behold wondrous things out of your law [Word]" (Psalm 119:18).

COMPONENTS OF YOUR MIND

1. The Intellect (The mind's "library") - The intellect has the capacity to comprehend knowledge and utilize it in thought. It is the power to learn and make connections.
2. Imagination (The mind's "eye") - The imagination has the capacity to conceive possibilities and generate new ideas within the mind, and visualize them internally. It is the power to create mental images.
3. Memory (The mind's "flash drive") - Memory has the ability to retrieve information stored in the mind, including experiences, events, feelings, and thoughts. It is the power to recollect.
4. Emotion (The mind's "voice") - Emotions enable us to experience inner passions in connection with particular

events, memories, experiences, or thoughts. They give us the power to feel. Emotions are the voice of our thoughts, communicating what and how we are thinking. They can also arise in response to physical events occurring within the body, such as hormonal changes, illness, or various stressors.

5. Reason/Will (The mind's "judge") - The will enables us to think about information, formulate judgments between conflicting options, viewpoints, or courses of action, and initiate action by the mind or body. It is the power to make decisions and act upon them.

You are what you think that

"As he thinks in his heart, so is he" (Proverbs 23:7).

Whatever we allow to captivate our thought life will eventually control our lives. The life we experience today is essentially a result of our thought life in the past. Proverbs 4:23 emphasizes the importance of guarding our hearts, as it determines the course of our lives. Whatever we continually meditate upon will begin to shape our reasoning, emotions, and will. Over time, we may unconsciously make choices to speak and act in ways that align with the prevailing thoughts in our minds.

Simultaneously, our thoughts carry the force of attraction. As we develop patterns of thinking, we begin to draw experiences, events, people, and resources into our lives that resonate with our thought patterns. This phenomenon is consistently observed and confirmed by almost all world religions, philosophies, and sociological observers.

The great news about this law of the mind is that if you don't just like the condition of your life, you'll change it. If you modify your mind, you modify your life.

Your Mind is Your Responsibility

As we have previously discussed, it has become common for people today to deny their responsibility for their thoughts, feelings, and actions. By doing so, we are disempowering ourselves from creating genuine change. We must recognize that our thoughts are our responsibility, and although we cannot control every thought that arises, we alone are accountable for what we allow to influence our minds. It is essential to take responsibility for our thoughts and feelings.

The first step to renewing your mind is to take ownership of your thought life. The reality is that we cannot change anything that we refuse to accept responsibility for. It is essential to become aware of what and how we think, as this is a crucial first step towards developing a new mind that aligns with the plans and purposes of God. Are there any limiting or defeating thoughts that you find yourself repeatedly returning to throughout the day? When you are alone with your thoughts, do you notice any patterns of thinking that your mind tends to drift towards? Are you keeping your life busy with activities to avoid confronting your thoughts, feelings, and fears? These are all signs that you need to regain control of your thought life. Begin by declaring the following confession of faith aloud:

In Jesus' name, I take full responsibility for my own mind. I exercise authority over my thoughts, feelings, meditations, and imagination. I acknowledge that I am the one who chooses which thoughts and mental images I allow to play on the screen of my mind. I will not let Satan force or intimidate me to think, feel, or meditate on anything that I do not permit. I recognize that my mind is a gift from God, and I choose to fill it with thoughts that will lead me into the life that God has planned for me.

Evaluate Your Thinking Life by Checkmating Your Feelings

Feelings are a result of our thoughts. One of the simplest ways to assess the state of our mind is to maintain a journal of negative and fearful thoughts that arise throughout the day. Just jot down words or phrases that reflect any thoughts or feelings that naturally come to your mind. By writing them down, you can get them out of your mind and onto paper, where you can evaluate them objectively. One or two days of doing this should be sufficient. You'll likely be surprised by how often your mind drifts towards fear, anger, lust, pride, jealousy, and self-condemnation. This is the wilderness of the human mind that has not been renewed in Christ. However, don't let this exercise discourage you.

After you have recorded a few days' worth of thoughts, review each one and ask yourself how you can think differently about them. Ask questions such as, "Is this thought valid? Is it worth surrendering control over my mind to think like this? How else could I view this situation? Is dwelling on this thought bringing about any positive change? What would happen if I replaced this negative thought with something positive and hopeful?

Next, create a quick list of three to five positive things that you want in your life and how you can manifest them. Then, ask yourself, "What if I spent my time thinking about these things instead?" This exercise is effective because it promotes self-awareness and enables you to take control of what you allow into your mind's stage.

The Process of Reprogramming

The modern computer is a marvel of human progress, but it was conceived, designed, and produced as a reproduction of the human mind in almost every way. Consider this: a computer has three basic elements — a monitor, a CPU (central processing unit), and an operator (programmer). For the purpose of this illustration, let's consider these three components as metaphors for the human spirit, soul, and body. The monitor represents the natural or physical life, the operator symbolizes the spirit, and the CPU represents the human soul or mind.

RENEWING YOUR MIND

Before we knew Christ, we were using an old operating system. Lost and misguided, we programmed our minds with all kinds of wrong things—bad language, bad behavior, bad shortcuts, and we had some really bad habits when it came to surfing the web of life. This filled our CPU with ungodly material. Then, one day, we were born again. A fresh, righteous, and spiritually alive operator was placed behind the same old computer and instructed to display new images and results on the screen. However, because the CPU had already been programmed and operated by the previous user, it still produces those bad images. Whenever we try to "surf the web" of our minds, the old habits, bookmarks, and historical data of the previous user keep popping up. The old programs are still running behind the scenes even though new applications or thoughts are installed.

Furthermore, viruses and spyware from all around the world continuously attempt to invade and corrupt our new applications. At times, the entire system crashes, and we revert to our old ways of thinking, speaking, and behaving. Fortunately, God has provided us with a unique "recovery system" that can always restart and restore our minds. This system comprises prayer, confession of sins, and trust in God's Word.

The only way to consistently alter what is being displayed on the screen of our lives is to reprogram our minds. We must carefully locate old files, eliminate them, and substitute them with new data. Initially, as we examine the results on the screen, we may be inclined to believe that nothing has altered. However, if we persist with the process, discarding the old and replacing it with new and beneficial information, eventually, the screen will exhibit what the programmer intends. We will begin to see the reflection of Jesus in ourselves.

This is a significant part of living a transformed life. We must give ourselves over to the task of deleting the old programmer's files, applications, and history, while simultaneously replacing them with new files and applications that reflect our new life in Christ. Just because your screen keeps displaying old programs doesn't mean you haven't changed; it just means you need to renew your CPU—your mind.

If your thoughts are fixed on God, His Word, and you trust Him together with your problems, you'll have real inner peace.

The Law of Exchange

God's Word doesn't just tell us what we shouldn't believe. Renewing your mind isn't about emptying your mind and using willpower to keep wrong thoughts out. That's an almost impossible task. The biblical concept of renewing your mind involves a spiritual principle that we'll call the law of exchange. According to this law, life operates on a continuous stream of "trades" or exchanges. You trade something you have in order to get something else. For instance, a student trades their time, attention, finances, and efforts to a university in exchange for knowledge that will help them achieve their goals in life and a diploma that confirms they have completed the outlined degree. Similarly, a man trades his bachelorhood for a committed relationship with his wife, in order to experience the joy of marriage and family. Every day, we all make decisions to trade our thoughts, time, energy, and attention to places, people, and things. These decisions shape the life we are currently living.

The life you are living today is essentially the result of the choices you have made in the past, regarding your time, talents, diet, money, words, friends, and thoughts. If you are not satisfied with the results – in other words, if you want to change some part of your current life – you will need to make different choices. This might seem too simple, but the key to changing your life is not more complicated than making the right choices. The moment you were born again, you exchanged your old, negative, sinful state of heart for a new heart that is softened by the grace, love, and life of Jesus. Renewing your mind is God's way of extending the life of Jesus into every area of your life and relationships.

Developing New Mindsets

If, then, you were raised with Christ, seek those things which are above, where Christ is seated at the right hand of God. Set your mind on things above, not on things on the earth." (Colossians 3:1-2)

SOBER

"For those who live according to the flesh set their minds on the things of the flesh, but those who live according to the Spirit set their minds on the things of the Spirit" (Romans 8:5).

In these verses, Paul is urging us to replace our worldly thought patterns with Christ-centered thinking. He instructs us to "set our minds" on things that are in line with the Spirit. Mindsets are not just fleeting thoughts or ideas; they are deeply ingrained patterns of thinking that develop over time. They are the result of consistently dwelling on a particular perspective until it becomes a habit for us.

Changing mindsets can be challenging, especially if they are deeply ingrained. However, having positive, helpful mindsets that align with the Word of God can bring great peace and strength. To change negative mindsets, we must replace our old thoughts with new ones. We should immerse ourselves in the truth of God's Word and consistently focus on right images until they replace our old mindsets. Paul continues in the following verses to instruct believers on the kinds of negative, worldly thoughts and behaviors that they need to "put off," and the new thoughts and actions they need to "put on.

But now you yourselves are to put off all these: anger, wrath, malice, blasphemy, and filthy language out of your mouth. Don't mislead each other, since you have put off the old man with his deeds and have put on the new man who is renewed in knowledge according to the image of Him who created him. Therefore, as the elect of God, holy and beloved, put on tender mercies, kindness, humility, meekness, and longsuffering. But above all these things, put on love, which is the bond of perfection. And let the peace of God rule in your hearts, to which also you were called in one body, and be thankful. Let the word of Christ dwell in you richly in all wisdom, teaching and admonishing one another in psalms and hymns and spiritual songs, singing with grace in your hearts to the Lord" (Colossians 3:8-10, 12, 14-16).

FEEDING ON THE WORD

By far, the most important tool we have to renew our minds is the Word of God. The Bible is filled with God's thoughts and ways (Isaiah 55:8-11). It has the power to heal our toxic thinking and deliver our minds from destructive patterns of belief and feeling.

If we can change our minds, we can change our lives. And if we can change our lives, God can change the world through us! "Humbly accept the word God has planted in your hearts, for it has the power to save [heal and deliver] your souls [minds]" (James 1:21 NLT). God's Word is a mirror of how He sees us in Christ. The New Testament letters written to the churches are filled with powerful images of what God has done for believers in Jesus. They describe repeatedly what we have become "in Christ." These letters tell us who we are in Christ and reveal our true identity. The more we look into the mirror of God's Word, the more we will see ourselves as God sees us - new creatures in Christ Jesus (2 Corinthians 5:17).

When we look at ourselves in a regular mirror, we only see our physical appearance. We may notice imperfections, mistakes, and things we want to change. However, God's Word gives us the true picture of who we really are. As believers in Jesus, we have been created in God's image and possess His love, peace, and wisdom. In our spirits, we have been given His divine nature - the very life of God! He has made us more than conquerors and given us authority over all the power of the enemy. This image is what God desires for us to capture in our minds. He wants us to comprehend in our minds what He has already made us to be in our hearts!

WAYS TO PREY ON GOD'S WORD

Jesus said, "Man does not live by bread alone, but by every word that comes from the mouth of God" (Matthew 4:4). Just as our bodies depend on natural bread for strength and nourishment, our spirits and souls need to feed on the spiritual food of God's Word. The Bible teaches us that there are many ways to consume God's Word, and each one is crucial for our development as believers.

The Teaching of the Local Church

The first way we receive God's Word is by regularly hearing it taught within the local church. In the early days of

Christianity, this was the only way to access God's Word. It took centuries before complete copies of the Bible could be found in most churches, and even more centuries before it was printed in smaller copies and made available to everyone. God created us to gather with other believers weekly in local churches so that we could be taught the Word of God under the guidance of His anointed preachers and teachers and allow His spiritual gifts to minister to the rest of the body. The primary responsibility of a local church pastor is to feed the flock a diet of God's Word. These passages make it clear that the pastors of God's church are responsible for teaching God's people.

"Remember them which have the rule over you, who have spoken unto you the word of God: whose faith follow, considering the end of their conversation." (Hebrews 13:7).

"So guard yourselves and God's people. Feed and shepherd God's flock— his church, purchased together with his own blood—over which the Holy Ghost has appointed you as elders" (Acts 20:28 NLT).

Personal Bible Reading and Group Study

Secondly, every believer should seek to study the Bible and good biblical teaching materials, both individually and in groups. When we read and study the Bible on our own, we allow the Holy Spirit to speak through the Scripture into our lives, using the stories, lessons, and teachings to help us think correctly. By participating in a Bible study that is led by the local church, we can gain a deeper understanding of God's

Word in an accelerated way. Often, believers help each other grow by learning from the insights that others are receiving from God's Word.

Memorizing Scripture

One of the most powerful ways to internalize God's Word is to commit helpful Bible verses to memory. While this may seem challenging, the reality is that the average person has already memorized thousands of lines and verses from songs, movies, and popular media. Memorizing the Bible may require some discipline and focus, but there is no song in the world that can benefit you more than God's Word. Psalm 119 is the longest chapter in the Bible, and each verse celebrates the power of God's Word in the believer's heart and life. It instructs us to commit God's Word to memory. Take note of these selected verses:

Thy word have I hidden in my heart that I might not sin against thee... I will meditate on thy precepts and have respect for thy ways. I will delight myself in thy statutes and not forget thy word... I will never forget thy precepts, for with them thou hast quickened me... MEM. How I love thy law! It is my meditation all day... Thy testimonies I have taken as my heritage forever, for they are the rejoicing of my heart... I have gone astray like a lost sheep; seek thy servant, for I do not forget thy commandments." (Psalm 119:11, 15-16, 93, 97, 111, 176 KJV).

RENEWING YOUR MIND

Bible Teaching Materials, Conferences, and Media

There are several excellent resources available today for learning and developing in God's Word. You can search for books, e-books, podcasts, digital downloads, videos, and other media that specialize in Bible teaching by reputable ministers who support learning that aligns with what you're experiencing and learning in your local church. However, it's important to remember that supplemental teaching should encourage you to be faithful to God and your local church. Any teaching that causes division among fellow believers or pulls you away from living your Christian life within a healthy local church community is contrary to God's purpose for you and should be viewed with caution.

Healing Your Memories

Renewing your mind involves healing your past, which is one of the most important aspects of this process. Memory is a powerful component of the human mind, and it has a significant impact on how we think and feel about our lives and our future. We live in a world that is filled with pain and brokenness, and as a result, we all have experiences that scar our memories. Whether it's the lack of love and affirmation we didn't receive or the rejection and abuse we didn't deserve, we all develop thinking patterns that grow like connective tissue around these unhealed wounds. Often, it takes years—sometimes until we reach physical adulthood—before we confront our painful memories and realize how they have impacted our thoughts, feelings, and decisions. In Psalm 23:1, 3, David says, "The LORD is my shepherd; I shall not want. He restores my soul: he leads me in the paths of righteousness for his name's sake."

As a saved believer in Jesus, your spirit has been made new. However, your soul may still contain unhealed hurts and patterns of thinking and feeling that are contrary to the love, joy, and peace that God has placed in your spirit. By following Christ and serving others within the local church, we embark on a journey that gradually brings many of those wounds and past hurts to the surface. When this happens, God's desire is to heal our soul and provide us with a new perspective that enables us to believe in both our past and our future.

Getting Unstuck

Sometimes, we may experience a decline in our spiritual growth, where our minds become stuck in patterns of thinking and feeling that prevent us from moving forward. In such instances, it's crucial to take the time to reflect on our thoughts and emotions. Often, the reason we feel "trapped" is because God wants us to examine the old patterns of thinking that we have picked up in the past and that are hindering us.

The Importance of latest Relationships

Building healthy relationships with other believers is a crucial aspect of spiritual growth and renewing our minds. When we embark on new directions, we need people to journey with us. Often, this requires us to let go of relationships that tie us to our past ways of thinking. It's like wanting to go to California but staying on a bus that's heading to Boston. God uses people who are heading in the direction of our purpose and destiny to help us reach the right places in life. When believers genuinely care for one another, share their hearts and hurts, and take the time to encourage and pray for each other, an environment for growth is created in our lives.

Christian Counseling

Sometimes, our minds and emotions can become so troublesome that we need help to heal. God works through His Word, His Spirit, His Church, and people to assist us in growing. Trained professionals such as ministers, counselors, and doctors have spent their lives learning how to help people heal their minds and emotions. Sometimes, God's plan for our growth involves spending time with wise and well-trained mature individuals who are called to this type of ministry. If you, your family, or your spiritual leaders feel that you may need this type of help, it is essential to locate someone who has a Christian-based worldview.

When the Brain is Sick

The brain is the organ that houses the human soul and mind. Like any other part of the body, it can become exhausted, overworked, imbalanced, or physically ill. However, unlike most other parts of our bodies, when our brains become imbalanced or sick, we often do not realize it.

SOBER

The brain is a complex network of chemical, hormonal, and electrical signals that can become unbalanced. This imbalance can manifest in ways that we do not typically associate with brain health. We may experience confusion in our thinking, depression in our emotions, disrupted sleep patterns, or fluctuating weight. It can become challenging to think clearly and control our impulses.

When the brain is weakened or ill due to stress, trauma, hormonal imbalances, or other issues, we need to give ourselves permission to seek the help we need to heal. In the Bible, when God's prophet Elijah had finished a particularly intense time of ministry, he became vulnerable to the threats of his enemies. Elijah was so exhausted that he lost his ability to think and feel well. He ran away and hid in a cave on a mountain, eventually praying for death. Along the way, the Lord allowed him to rest, had angels prepare food to revive him, and eventually helped him out of his depression by sending a personal assistant to help Elijah carry his burdens. This demonstrates the great mercy of God for His people when they fall into places of exhaustion and toxic thinking.

In Jonah chapter four, we see that God's prophet became despondent and fixated on negative thoughts. Things did not go as he had hoped, and he even prayed for God to take his life. However, instead of granting Jonah's request, God gently corrected his perspective and taught him a valuable lesson. God shifted Jonah's thinking, which ultimately changed how he felt.

Sometimes, healing the brain may involve changes in diet, sleep patterns, stress levels, and medication. A believer should not feel condemned if they discover that God's plan for their healing includes counseling or medical treatment as part of renewing their minds. The most crucial aspect is that we take necessary steps to attain healthy brains, healthy minds, and healed memories and emotions.

The renewing of the mind is the most significant factor in living a transformed life. If we can change our minds, we can change our lives. When we change our lives, God can work through us to transform the world!

STEPS TO RENEW YOUR MIND

Apostle Paul stated in Romans 12:2, "And be not conformed to this world: but be ye transformed by the renewing of your mind, that ye may prove what is that good, and acceptable, and perfect, will of God". Many of us mistakenly believe that our minds will be renewed immediately after our lives are transformed. However, it's actually the opposite. When we were born, most of us emerged headfirst into this world. If you want to escape terrible circumstances, professional limitations, or stagnation in ministry, your head has to come out first.

SOBER

When you experience freedom, your mindset has to shift from that of a slave to that of a son or soldier. Even if you face similar challenges as before, you'll be able to view them from a different perspective. I like to remind our church that "You are not a sick person trying to get healed; you are a healthy person fighting sickness." "You are not a bound person trying to get free; you are a free person fighting captivity." "You are not a sinner trying to become a saint; you are a saint fighting sin."

<u>Step 1:</u> Stop expecting an outdoor miracle to change your mind. The largest part of these miracles will never come until you get rid of the pandemonium in your mind by filling it with God's Word. Renewing of the mind will never work if someone believes the excuse, "The reason why my mind is so negative is that my life is so hard." Have you ever considered that perhaps the reason your life is so hard is that your mind is so negative? You cannot have miracles in your life regularly if your mind is a mess. Do not get me wrong, we need miracles, but they alone cannot change our minds without our humility and willingness to make God's Word the standard for our lives. Remember, a corresponding sun that melts the ice also hardens the clay. Miracles are like that for those who are hungry for God's Word. Miracles help our faith, but for those who are refusing God's Word to have dominion over their lives, miracles are never enough. If you stop blaming your circumstances for your negative thinking, God will start working on you in a powerful way.

RENEWING YOUR MIND

Step 2: Stop believing that you cannot control your thoughts. The second lie that must be rejected is, "I cannot control my thoughts, they control me." This is a weak excuse and not Scriptural. The Bible commands us to "think on these things: whatsoever things are true, whatsoever things are honest, whatsoever things are just, whatsoever things are pure, whatsoever things are lovely, whatsoever things are of good report; if there be any virtue, and if there be any praise" (Philippians 4:8), "You shall meditate thereon day and night" (Joshua 1:8), "On His law he meditates day and night" (Psalm 1:2). It is clear that God expects us to choose our thoughts, not let our thoughts be controlled by something else. Practically speaking, we do get attacked in our minds because our minds are a battlefield, not a playground. When a Christian connects their spirit with the Holy Ghost, their spirit becomes stronger. When the spirit is weak, the mind runs tasks for the flesh by thinking negative thoughts. But as we constantly build our spirit by communing with the Holy Ghost, our mind comes under the influence of the Word of God and the Holy Ghost who lives in us. We are then left with the choice to think on God's things or let our mind go with the flow of life.

Step 3: What you feed your mind with becomes your mindset. Your mindset is difficult to change without altering the content that your mind is filled with. Often, when we hear about breaking strongholds or renewing our minds, we become motivated to change our mindsets. However, we soon realize that this is not an easy task. The only way to transform your default and automatic thinking is by intentionally filling your conscious mind with new information that aligns with God's truth. As your conscious mind becomes saturated with this information, it eventually spills over into your subconscious mind.

Step 4: Confess what you believe, not what you feel. Our confessions have the power to shape our reality. We receive salvation by confessing Jesus as the Lord of our lives, and we obtain God's promises by speaking them out loud. When we only confess what we feel or see, we hinder our faith and allow negative thoughts to persist. Just as Jesus did in the wilderness during His temptation with the Devil, we must combat negative thoughts with Scripture by speaking it aloud. Don't be tempted to merely think the Scripture, speak it out loud instead. This is how we can change our minds and renew our thinking patterns. Therefore, learn to confess God's word instead of what you feel or see.

Step 5. Resist negative thoughts, assist positive thoughts. Positive thoughts don't get to stay; they have to be assisted. Negative thoughts don't get to leave; they have to be resisted. We must support the Word of God by making room for it in our hearts and resist the evil thoughts of the enemy by taking them captive and bringing them into submission to Christ (see 2 Corinthians 10:5). You cannot stop birds from flying over your head, but you can prevent them from building a nest in your hair. Bad thoughts may come, but they don't have to stay if we speak against them with the truth of God's Word.

Step 6. Celebrate the process. It takes time to see change in your mind. I believe there's a reason why God took six days to create the world instead of doing it in one day. He wanted to show us how to go through the process of change. Each day, something great was accomplished, and God would end the day by celebrating what was done, instead of complaining about what was still unfinished. On the third day, even though there was still a lot of work to be done, God saw that it was good. He didn't focus on what was still unfinished. Although there was much left to do, He celebrated what had been completed.

"It's also worth noting that God never compared the messy process of creation to the beautiful heaven where He resides. The Devil will try to ruin the process of renewing your mind by making you compare your progress with someone else's. You are complete in God, and you don't need to compare yourself to others. Comparing leads to complaining, and complaining can cause you to break the tenth commandment of coveting. Covetousness kills the creative process of God in renewing your mind. If your neighbor's lawn looks greener than yours, start watering your own lawn. Be the best version of yourself that the world has ever seen. Remember, what God started, He is faithful to complete (see Philippians 1:6). He is not finished with you yet."

Step 7. Expect miracles. Expecting something good to happen is a choice; it's an act of faith. Individuals with a renewed mind have positive expectations at the forefront of their minds. Don't let your imagination create a negative picture where things go wrong, such as sickness worsening, relationships breaking, or businesses failing. Instead, replace those negative thoughts with promises from the Word of God. Some people wake up in the morning with a sense that something bad will happen to them that day. If this happens to you, it's from the Devil. Go back to bed and try again until you have a positive feeling that God is good, and He plans good things for you.

If you continue to have negative thoughts and they become a reality, you are releasing your faith for your own trouble. Instead, choose to trust in God and expect His grace and mercy, not accidents, tickets, or chaos. This doesn't mean that we will never have bad days, but we should not live expecting them. Remember that the quality of your thoughts determines the happiness in your life. Vance Havner once said, "God uses broken things. It takes broken soil to produce a crop, broken clouds to give rain, broken grain to give bread, broken bread to give strength. It is the broken alabaster box that gives forth perfume. It is Peter, weeping bitterly, who returns to greater power than ever." So, renew your mind and focus on positive thoughts.

CHAPTER SEVEN

STRENGTHENING THE MIND

Ephesians 3:16 says "hat he would grant you, according to the riches of his glory, to be strengthened with might by his Spirit in the inner man;"

Your mind is a territory that must be conquered. Hope is crucial in igniting and sustaining the power of your mind. Life will inevitably present its ups and downs, attempting to knock us off course, but a fortified mind built on hope can persevere until victory is achieved. Tough times are temporary, but resilient individuals with strong minds endure. Yielding to self-pity and succumbing to destructive behaviors is a sign of cowardice in the battle of the mind. Regardless of the challenges we face, hope for a better tomorrow and the strength to persevere are what drive us forward. To strengthen your mind, you must cultivate and nurture hope.

What is Hope?

Judith Rich once said, "Hope is a match in a dark tunnel, a moment of light, just enough to reveal the path ahead and ultimately the way out." The definition of hope varies depending on the person speaking. In a spiritual context, hope may involve faith in a higher power and belief that good things will happen. Individuals may direct their hopes outward through prayer to God. For others, hope may involve maintaining a positive outlook and seeing challenges as opportunities. According to Merriam-Webster, the definition of "hope" can seem similar to "wish": "to cherish a desire with anticipation: to want something to happen or be true."

Whatever the details, hope generally means a desire for things to improve, and to work towards a better situation. When you're in the midst of an agonizingly painful situation, it's easy to focus on your suffering and lose sight of the bright ray of hope emerging on your horizon. If your world is falling apart, the difficulties you're experiencing can be overwhelming. Every thought is filtered through a sieve of pain, pressure, and misery. Hope is the key to strengthening your mind; otherwise, the mind can become lost and lead to despair. Sobriety is more effective when there is hope.

There are numerous resources available on what the Bible has to say about strengthening and renewing our minds, submitting our thoughts, and bringing them into captivity. God's Word contains several principles related to our mind, which is our greatest asset. These principles help guide and control our thoughts. In this piece, I will delve into what I consider to be pertinent regarding these topics.

STRENGTHENING THE MIND

1) NOT EVERYTHING YOU THINK SHOULD BE BELIEVED

It is common to assume that our thoughts are genuine simply because they come from within us. However, the fact that we think something does not necessarily make it true. I have seen firsthand the face of mental illness and the diversity of suggestions that can arise in the mind. False ideas are constantly bombarding us from the world, and Satan also makes suggestions all the time. However, our predicament is much more profound than that of Satan. All human beings suffer from mental issues, and this mental illness is called sin. The Bible uses a number of different phrases to describe the condition of our minds under sin, including confusion (Deuteronomy 28:20), anxiety, closed (Job 17:3–4), evil, restlessness (Ecclesiastes 2:21–23), rashness, and delusion (Leviticus 5:4; Isaiah 32:4 NIV). The Bible also describes different kinds of minds, such as a troubled mind (2 Kings 6:11), a depraved mind (1 Timothy 6:5), a sinful mind (Romans 8:7 NIV), a dull mind (2 Corinthians 3:14 NIV), a blinded mind (2 Corinthians 4:4), and a corrupt mind (2 Timothy 3:8).

Our Broken Minds

Our minds are wrecked by sin, which means we cannot depend even on what we think, ourselves. As Jeremiah 17:9 states, "The heart is deceitful above all things, and desperately wicked: who can know it?" We have a remarkable ability to deceive ourselves and deny obvious realities. We may convince ourselves that things are not as bad as they truly are, or that things are better than they really are. We may believe that we are doing well when we are actually struggling, or that something is not a big deal when it truly is. The truth is, according to Scripture, we cannot trust ourselves to tell the truth. This is all the more reason to question our own thoughts and to teach others not to believe everything they think.

Just because you have a thought does not mean it is accurate. This is one of the reasons why we have a lot of fallen Christian leaders, because all sin begins with a lie. Worse still, the Bible says Satan is 'the father of lies' (John 8:44). And if he can get you to believe a lie, he can get you to sin. Above all, self-will can cause God to renounce an individual and also cause them to believe a lie. 2 Thessalonians 2:9-11 says, 'Even him, whose coming is after the working of Satan with all power and signs and lying wonders, And with all deceivableness of unrighteousness in them that perish; because they received not the love of the truth, that they might be saved. And for this cause, God shall send them strong delusion, that they should believe a lie.' Anytime an individual sins, it is a thought of knowing better than God. God said this particular thing, but what about that? And consequently, you have to question what you think. 1 John 1:8 (KJV) says, 'If we say we have no sin, we deceive ourselves, and the truth is not in us.' We constantly deceive ourselves most of the time.

Preconditioned to Misunderstand

I have noticed that in another era, genuineness was highly valued. I would like to ask, when has inauthenticity ever been fashionable? Genuineness has always been an appealing quality. However, some people who promote their genuineness are not truly aware of what it means. You are not authentic until you can freely admit how often you are inauthentic. Authenticity begins when you acknowledge your own inauthenticity. We all have blind spots, some of us have more than others, but we all have them. We cannot always tell ourselves the truth because we do not take the time to truly think. Often, we make snap judgments and fail to notice important details. We all have more underlying biases than we realize, and we jump to conclusions. The scripture talks about this in Romans 2. We get caught up in categories, asking ourselves, 'Are you this or that?' when, in reality, there are not only two or three categories. One significant reason why we should not accept everything we think is that we tend to see what we want to see. Having studied the brain extensively, I recently learned that the optic nerve, which is the only nerve that goes directly to the brain, actually sends more signals from the brain forward than from the eye backward. This means that our brain is telling us what we see, and we are already preconditioned to interpret it in a certain way. That's why if you put four people at an accident scene, each of them will see something different. Therefore, we must remind ourselves and teach others not to accept everything we think.

2) GUARD YOUR MIND FROM GARBAGE

The second thing to understand in the fight for the mind is the importance of guarding it against rubbish. The ancient cliché from the early days of computing - GIGO, garbage in/garbage out - still holds true today. Just as putting bad information into a computer results in poor output, filling your mind with mental trash can lead to negative outcomes in your life. Proverbs 15:14 states, "The heart of him that hath understanding seeketh knowledge: but the mouth of fools feedeth on foolishness" (KJV). This is a great verse to write on a Post-it note and attach to your TV, as a reminder the next time you consider watching something.

Just as there are different types of nourishment for the physical body, there are also different types of nourishment for the brain. Brain nourishment helps make you smarter, while junk food provides empty calories. Toxic nourishment, on the other hand, can be harmful. Keep this in mind the next time you decide what to feed your mind.

The same is true for what you see, hear, and allow into your mind. Some things are brain nourishment, which can make you smarter, more virtuous, and emotionally mature. Then there's junk food, which is just filling and neither good nor bad, as 1 Corinthians has 6:12 said, "All things are lawful unto me, but all things are not expedient: all things are lawful for me, but I will not be brought under the power of any." In other words, some things aren't necessarily wrong, but they aren't essential. The Bible tells us to fill our minds with the right things if we want to be healthy, successful in our Christian life, and in serving others. Set your mind on the right things to be effective in your service.

By the way, some people say, "God hasn't called me to be fruitful. He's called me to be faithful." That's simply not true. The Bible says that God expects not only faithfulness but also productivity. Follow it through the Bible texts: "Ye have not chosen me, but I have chosen you, and ordained you, that ye should go and bring forth fruit, and that your fruit should remain: that whatsoever ye shall ask of the Father in my name, he may give it you" (John 15:16). Jesus even cursed a fig tree because it didn't bear fruit.

It is clear that you would never invite someone over to your home and ask them to commit an immoral act before you. However, each time you watch a TV program that includes infidelity, you are essentially doing just that. Similarly, you would never invite someone to kill someone in your living room, but you are essentially doing so each time you watch a TV scene where people are being murdered.

It is important to safeguard your mind against harmful content. How do you ensure that you are not exposing your mind to trash? How can you help others protect their minds against waste? Some individuals believe that they can allow anything into their mind and still be fine. However, this is not true, and those who are too open-minded risk losing their ability to think clearly.

Therefore, it is important to be mindful of the content you consume and to make a conscious effort to avoid harmful material. Additionally, it is important to help others understand the importance of protecting their minds from negative influences. Remember, what you feed your mind will determine the type of person you become.

Ways to Protect Our Minds

Philippians 4:6–8 provides us two ways to guard our minds from garbage which are conversational prayer and concentrated focusing (Heads):

Be careful for nothing; but in everything, by prayer and supplication with thanksgiving, let your requests be made known unto God. And the peace of God, which passeth all understanding, shall keep your hearts and minds through Christ Jesus. Finally, brethren, whatsoever things are true, whatsoever things are honest, whatsoever things are just, whatsoever things are pure, whatsoever things are lovely, whatsoever things are of good report; if there be any virtue, and if there be any praise, think on these things. (KJV)

How does one know when they have the peace that "surpasses all understanding"? It happens once you stop trying to fully understand why God does what He does and begin to trust Him easily. This tranquility "will guard your hearts and minds.

The first way to guard your heart and mind is to wish for everything. Then, Paul says to believe in "whatever is true, whatever is honorable, whatever is just, whatever is pure, whatever is lovely, and whatever is commendable, if there is any excellence, if there is anything worthy of praise." He says to wish for everything. If you were to wish as much as you worry, you would have a lot less to stress about. Don't worry about anything, but pray about everything. This type of prayer is like a running conversation, which means we don't have to be on our knees or close our eyes.

I have trained myself to do this. I ask God all the time. I'm even talking to Him while writing to you. You'll develop a two-track mind. The average person can speak 150 words per minute, but the typical mind can understand about 350 words per minute -- that's a 200-word per minute boredom factor. So, you can ask God and talk to somebody else at the same time. That's why you should pray about everything and maintain a running conversation with Him.

Second, Paul says that we should always fix our thoughts. Thinking about this statement, how does one do that? By focusing. This is often one of the keys to overcoming the feeling of wanting to do something: don't only resist it; replace it. Whatever you simply resist continues to exist. The more you strike a nail, the harder you drive it into the wood. And when people say "I don't want to believe this," what are they doing? They are sadly thinking about it! And whatever gets your focus gets you. James tells us that "sin when it's matured creates death" (James 1:15). So don't only resist it.

When I was a young kid and knew my mother had baked cookies, I would go up to the edge of the kitchen counter, and she would say, "Now, Ricky, don't eat those cookies." I would say, "I'm not, Mom. I'm just looking." I'm looking. I don't want it. I don't want it. Then I would grab it and eat it. Don't just resist; replace. Change the channel. Refocus. In the words of Thomas Chalmers, it's "the expulsive power of a new affection" that turns your mind away from the things that the Devil wants you to focus on and toward the things that God wants you to focus on. Protect your mind from garbage, and that is the second key.

3) CONTINUE LEARNING

The third thing to find out and teach to others during this fight for the mind is to never stop learning. Become a lifelong learner. Love knowledge. Love wisdom. Learn to enjoy the act of learning. The word 'loyal student' means 'learner.' You can't be a loyal student of Christ without being a learner. Jesus said, 'Come to me, all who are weary and burdened, and I will give you rest. Take my yoke upon you, and learn from me' (Matthew 11:28-29). What does one do once they combat a yoke? They share an important responsibility with another animal. They lighten a load. And Jesus wants us to learn from him.

STRENGTHENING THE MIND

Many people act as though their education ended with their last graduation. I have even met pastors who haven't cracked open a book since their school days. They never studied anything or taken another class since then. Are you kidding me? To be a loyal student means to be a learner. All leaders must first be loyal students. So leaders must first be learners. The moment you stop learning, you stop leading. Growing churches require growing pastors. The moment you stop growing, your church stops growing.

You can learn from anybody if you only know the proper questions. The Bible says, 'Counsel in the heart of man is like deep water, but a man of understanding will draw it out' (Proverbs 20:5 KJV). In other words, you can learn from anybody if you only learn to tap into their knowledge. And how do you do it? You draw it out by asking questions. We all know things that others don't, and others know things that we don't. That's why the Bible says, 'As iron sharpens iron, so one person sharpens another' (Proverbs 27:17).

Humility is essential

But if you're really committed to learning, you need one quality in particular: humility (not bragging). Why does God resist the proud and give grace to the humble (1 Peter 5:5)? Because the humble are teachable. I would rather admit that I don't understand everything than pretend that I do and refuse to learn. You can learn from anybody.

SOBER

I learn from churches larger than Saddleback. I learn from churches smaller than Saddleback. I learn from people older than me and from those who are younger. I learn from people who don't like me. I even learn from people who say bad things or have different opinions than me. I learn from people who totally misunderstand me. You can learn from anybody. Learning from your enemies can be a way to be smarter than them. Because if your enemies only learn from themselves, but you learn from them, then you'll know not only what they know but also what you know!

Proverbs 18:15 declared that the mind of a (reasonable/showing good judgment) person is interested in strongly encourage knowledge [that's a mark of intelligence!], and therefore the person (who gives opinions about what could or should be done about things) listens to find out more." we'd like to be wanting to learn and willing to (mainly study). Learn this old and boring (expression): "God gave us two ears and one mouth," so we should always listen twice the maximum amount as we speak. Proverbs 10:14 says, " Wise men layup knowledge: but the mouth of the foolish is near destruction." (KJV).

In Holy Scripture, knowledge is the only thing we can store up. Jesus says we should not store up money, treasure, or material possessions that can be destroyed by moth and rust. Instead, we should store up knowledge because it is more valuable than money. You can always earn more money, but knowledge is something you will take with you to heaven. You will leave all your worldly riches behind, but a wealth of knowledge goes with you.

Suggestions for Growing in Knowledge

One way to store up knowledge is to start a family library, a collection of godly books that can be passed down to future generations. In my family, four generations ago, our ancestors started a family library that was passed down to my dad, who then passed it down to me. When I was sixteen years old, I began collecting books and for many years I read a book every day. Today, I have thousands of books in my library.

As an adolescent, I heard, 'The impact on your life will mostly come from the people you meet and the books you read.' So, I decided to be intentional about both of these — whom I would meet and what I would read. And when you begin to build a library of godly, Christian books, you are leaving a legacy for future generations. Twice in the book of Proverbs, we are told to 'store up my commands within you' (Proverbs 2:1; 7:1 NIV). If you are going into eternity, you are going to take that with you. If you're sober about growing in knowledge and growing in your mind, here's the approach I put forward:

- Read 25 percent of your books from the first fifteen hundred years of church history. Many people tend to overlook the period between the time of Paul and Luther. However, God was at work during that time, and by ignoring the teachings of the early church, we are dismissing the work of God. We should remember that God was faithfully teaching His Word during those times as well.

- Read 25 percent from the last 500 years, since the Reformation.
- Read 25 percent from the last 100 years.
- Read only 25 percent from modern authors of the last ten years.

A lot of individuals know all the fashionable books and none of the classics. Jesus didn't just begin building his church within the year 2000. He has been working in and through his body for 2 millennia, and you'll save yourself tons of your time if you'll help yourself of availing yourself with these books. It is also easier! It saves tons of your time and saves us from making the mistakes of others.

Read, Read, Read

I make it a habit to read through the works of significant thinker every year. I read books by Edwards, I read books of Barth, as well books of Wesley and a few other leaders. It's important to remember that leaders from the past have much to teach us. There is nothing new under the sun, and any supposed new revelation is likely false because the truth is eternal. What was true a thousand years ago is still true today, and it will continue to be true a thousand years from now.

STRENGTHENING THE MIND

Truth is not something that is created, but rather something that is discovered. If God has revealed something as true, then it has been seen by someone else in the church before. In fact, if you ever come across a truth that no one else has ever seen, it's likely that you're mistaken.

The Bible says "Wise men store up knowledge" (Proverbs 10:14). And here's Proverbs 19:8: " He that getteth wisdom loveth his own soul: he that keepeth understanding shall find good." We must make time to think. Plan it in your life. Plan for a balance between doing and thinking. We'd like both of them in our lives.

Levels of Learning

Let me summary quickly what I call "the five levels of learning." I have been using this method for the past thirty years, and it has been instrumental in bringing numerous people into our church and sending many out to do ministry and mission work. I believe that a church's effectiveness should be measured not by its seating capacity but by its sending capacity.

The health of a military is not determined by how many soldiers sit in the mess hall and attend weekly Bible studies, but rather by how many are on the frontlines fighting in the world. Our goal should be to bring people into the church, build them up, train them, and then send them out to do the work of ministry. To achieve this, we must teach people not only to love the Word but also to live it out (James

1:22-25). I have developed a teaching method that I call 'the five levels of learning' which help us achieve this goal.

1) Knowledge
2) (way of seeing things / sensible view of what's and isn't important) (Wisdom)
3) Conviction
4) Character
5) Skill

The first two have to do with knowing. The second two have to do with being, and therefore the third one has to do with doing. You can use these as an example that should be followed for all of your loyal studentship, moving people from "come and see" to "come and die.

1) <u>Knowledge</u>

First, we would like to emphasize the importance of knowledge. As God says in Hosea 4:6, "My people are destroyed for lack of knowledge." When we are not familiar with the Word of God, we are at risk of being destroyed, and so it is essential for us to not only study the Bible but also learn about church history. That is why our church includes a figure from history, highlighting an individual's life story, in our weekly written announcements. Additionally, we share a spiritual word of the week, also included in our written announcements, to help people understand religious terminology and the great saints of church history. This is all part of gaining knowledge.

STRENGTHENING THE MIND

Unfortunately, it is possible to learn the scriptures without truly understanding their content; in other words, one can know all the facts without truly knowing the meaning. To truly know something, one must apply it in their life. This is why Jesus pointed out to the Pharisees that their issue was not a lack of knowledge of the Holy Scriptures, but a lack of understanding of the power of God (Mark 12:24).

It is remarkable to consider the strong rebuke that Jesus gave to the Pharisees, who had memorized the first five books of the Bible: Genesis, Exodus, Leviticus, Numbers, and Deuteronomy. Despite their knowledge, Jesus pointed out that their problem was a lack of true understanding of the scriptures. They needed to not only display their knowledge but also teach others to value learning and to counter those who opposed it. It is worth noting that there are many intelligent Christians today who are engaging in intellectual battles against the various competing ideas of the world, many of whom are much more brilliant than I am.

2) Perspective (Wisdom)

The second thing we need is insight, which the Bible refers to as "wisdom." Wisdom involves seeing life from God's perspective, understanding the reasons behind God's actions. Knowledge provides the foundation, while insight and wisdom are the building blocks that follow. Knowledge is knowing what God does, but insight is understanding why God does it.

Unfortunately, some churches excel in Bible knowledge but fail to teach their congregation insight and wisdom. As Isaiah 55:8 explains in The Message version of the Bible, God's ways and thoughts are beyond human comprehension: "I don't think the way you think. The way you work isn't the way I work." It is evident that this is true. Psalm 103:7 highlights the fact that the Lord revealed his ways to Moses, but only his deeds were made known to the children of Israel.

The children of Israel witnessed the acts of God, including miracles like the parting of the Red Sea, the water at Marah, the provision of doves and manna, and much more. However, while they had knowledge of these events, Moses had insight into the ways of God and understood the reasons behind His actions. While knowledge of the Word of God is important, the goal of perception is to develop the mind of God as much as possible. This involves cultivating the mind of Christ, as described in 1 Corinthians 2:14-16 and Philippians 2:5-11, for ourselves and others.

3) onviction

The third essential element is conviction. This forms the third building block, which relies on the foundation of knowledge and the development of insight into God's ways. As we deepen our understanding of the Word of God and gain insight into His motives and purposes, we begin to develop strong convictions.

STRENGTHENING THE MIND

Gaining perspective into God's view on temptation, evil, our past, present, and future, sin, and Satan can help us develop strong convictions. By understanding God's perspective on these issues, we can develop a solid foundation for our faith and conviction in His ways.

Conviction isn't opinion. Opinions are something you argue about; convictions are something you die for. And what we need today as much as ever are men and women of godly, biblical convictions. If you know hardly anything about history, you will still know that the people who have had the greatest impact on our world for good or evil were not the neatest, not those who had the most knowledge, not the wealthiest, not the most talented, but those who had the deepest convictions for right or wrong. And, of course, it's Jesus who has made the greatest impact, and it's Jesus who had the deepest convictions of all.

If you want to understand how much Jesus loves you, look at the cross. With arms outstretched and nail-pierced hands, Jesus shows us how much he and his Father love us. As it says in Romans 5:8, 'But God shows his love for us in that while we were still sinners, Christ died for us.' Jesus says, 'I love you so much it hurts. I love you so much that every drop of blood falling to the ground says, "I love you."' That's conviction.

Paul discusses in 1 Corinthians 7 about being settled in our own minds, which suggests having godly convictions.

And in Hebrews 11:1, faith is described as "the conviction of things not seen." Let me offer you some examples.

"For I am persuaded that neither death, nor life, nor angels, nor principalities, nor powers, nor things present, nor things to come, nor height, nor depth, nor any other creature, shall be able to separate us from the love of God, which is in Christ Jesus our Lord" (Romans 8:38-39). That's conviction. It is not a mere opinion; it is a conviction.

"And we know that all things work together for good to them that love God, to them who are the called according to his purpose. For whom he did foreknow, he also did predestinate to be conformed to the image of his Son, that he might be the firstborn among many brethren" (Romans 8:28-29). That's a conviction, not an opinion of any sort.

"I have shown you all things, how that so laboring ye ought to support the weak, and to remember the words of the Lord Jesus, how he said, It is more blessed to give than to receive" (Acts 20:35). That is a personal conviction.

"For the which cause I also suffer these things: nevertheless I am not ashamed: for I know whom I have believed, and am persuaded that he is able to keep that which I have committed unto him against that day" (2 Timothy 1:12 KJV). That is a conviction. We need people of conviction today.

And there is this grand conviction: "Though he slay me, yet will I trust in him: but I will maintain mine own ways before him" (Job 13:15 KJV). I do not need to bother if I understand it or not, Job says, but I am going to trust God no matter what.

In conviction, we need to have the heart of God. It is not just about seeing what God sees, but also about feeling what God feels - for the world, for the lost, for His Word, and for His church. We need to acquire knowledge, but we must also align ourselves with God's perspective. However, it is not enough to merely understand the mind of God; we must also be moved by the emotions that arise from that understanding.

4) <u>Character</u>

Once we begin to cultivate emotions, we start developing propensities, and the sum total of our propensities is what we call "character." We cannot claim to have the character of genuineness unless we consistently practice being genuine. We cannot claim to have the character of thoughtfulness unless we consistently demonstrate kindness. Character is the culmination of our habits. If I were to tell my spouse, "Honey, I'll be faithful to you twenty-nine days of the month," she knows, and I know, that partial faithfulness is still unfaithfulness. It is only true loyalty if it is my habitual tendency to always be faithful to her. We build character by developing the habits of love, joy, peace, patience, kindness, goodness, gentleness, faithfulness, and self-control, as outlined in Galatians 5:22-23. These are the fruits of the Spirit, which reflect the character of Christ. If we desire to become more like Jesus, then we must seek to manifest the fruits of the Spirit in our lives. The goal is to become more like God in our character, not to become gods ourselves. We will never become God, no matter how much progress we make. The idea that we can become like God is the oldest lie in the book, as mentioned in Genesis 3:5. Therefore, our focus should be on learning and developing character.

5) <u>Skill</u>

When we begin to develop our character and benefit habitually through daily Bible reading, regular fasting, consistent prayer, and frequent days of prayer and witnessing, these practices become ingrained habits in our lives. As we continue to consistently engage in them, we will become more proficient and skillful in these areas. Ultimately, we reach the highest level of learning, which is mastery of these practices.

Skill is developed through repetition and practice. Ecclesiastes 10:10 states, "If the iron is blunt, and one does not sharpen the edge, he must use more strength, but wisdom helps one to succeed." This is one of my "life verses." If you are chopping wood, having a sharp axe is crucial. With a dull axe, it takes more effort to chop the wood, but with a sharp one, less effort is needed. "Skill brings success." This verse does not suggest that prayer, desire, or dedication alone will bring success. Instead, it emphasizes the importance of developing skills. A farmer may pray all he wants, but if he tries to harvest a wheat field with a grape picker, he won't succeed. We need to have the right skills for the job at hand.

I know many men who are godly, love Jesus, and preach the Bible, but their churches are struggling. The Bible teaches that skill leads to success. We never waste our time when we sharpen our skills. That's why I challenge you to attend conferences and learn from anyone and everyone. We should not only know the Word of God but also seek to possess His mind, heart, and character, and to fulfill His desires. As James 1:22 says, 'Be doers of the word, and not hearers only'.

I've expressed this sentiment before, but I feel it's important to reiterate: what we need now is another Reformation. However, this time around, it must focus on actions, not just beliefs. Some have misunderstood my stance and accused me of disregarding creeds altogether, but this is not the case. In fact, I think deeply about creeds and frequently preach on them. The issue is not solely with creeds, but rather the fact that they must be put into practice. It's not a question of choosing between one or the other - both are necessary. We must not only teach sound doctrine but also demonstrate through our actions the behaviors that align with it. It's imperative that we become doers and actively live out the teachings of the Word.

The fact is, we only truly believe in the components of the Bible that we actually practice. For example, one might say, "I believe in witnessing." But if they do not actively engage in it, then they do not truly believe in it. Similarly, if someone says, "I believe in tithing," but does not practice it, then they do not truly believe in it. The same goes for believing in having family devotions; if one does not practice it, they do not truly believe in it. Essentially, we only believe what we actually put into action. Our main problem is that we possess a vast amount of knowledge, yet we fail to apply it. We also tend to teach others too much, to the point where they are unable to effectively apply it. It's important to keep in mind that overwhelming people with too much information can hinder their ability to put it into practice.

I grew up with parents who were deeply devoted to their religion. Every Sunday morning, the very first thing I did was attend Sunday school, where I was supposed to receive an application that would change my life. Then I would attend the morning service, and there, I would receive another application that was supposed to change my life. Later in the day, I would attend something called 'church training,' where I was expected to receive yet another life-changing application. And finally, in the evening service, there was yet another application intended to change my life.

That's four applications in one day! After that, I was supposed to attend midweek prayer and Bible study to receive yet another application. Maybe there would be a Thursday morning study where I could get another application. And then, I was expected to have a quiet time every day of the week, each with an application. That's about fourteen applications every week. Friend, our lives don't change that much that fast. I'm doing well if I can apply one good lesson every week. The problem in many of our churches is that before we truly apply last week's or this morning's message, we are already moving on to learn (or teach) something else.

We often take notes and fill notebooks, thinking that by writing things down, we are actually learning. But we are not. There is a significant gap between knowledge and action in Christianity, and perhaps the reason for this is too much teaching. We move on to the next thing before we have even applied what we have learned, and we cannot change that quickly. Another weakness of the church today when it comes to learning is that pastors often fail to teach their congregations how to feed themselves. We do all the feeding instead of showing the sheep how to feed themselves. We all need to learn how to do a scientific Bible study, a thematic study, and a book synthesis. How do we analyze a chapter? What are the steps involved in doing a word study? How do we conduct a biographical study? Often, we preachers preach about what people should do without giving them practical instructions on how to do it.

When I was growing up, my dad worked for the church, so I heard more sermons than most people. As I listened to these sermons and took notes, I found myself writing "YBH, YBH, YBH" - yes, but how? Without application, interpretation is meaningless. If we only teach people the theory without showing them how to put it into practice, we may end up with people who have big heads but tiny hearts, hands, and feet. Jesus showed us how to live by giving us practical instructions. In Isaiah 26:3, it says, "Thou wilt keep him in perfect peace, whose mind is stayed on thee: because he trusteth in thee." Our mental well-being depends on what we think about. Therefore, we should focus our minds on the Word of God, the mind of God, the values of God, the character of God, and the abilities of God.

4) LET GOD STRETCH YOUR IMAGINATION

Finally, before closing this chapter, let's discuss the importance of imagination. If we want to learn how to fight for the mind and teach others to do the same, we must learn how to allow God to expand our imaginations. This is a crucial part of the battle and of our thought process. Every event in life begins with a dream. Someone has to imagine it first.

This is a gift that God has given us: the power to dream, imagine, and visualize something before it becomes a reality. Every building we see was first imagined by a designer or builder before it was built. Every piece of art was imagined before it was painted, and every song was imagined before it was written. Every athletic award and every trophy was imagined by the athlete before it ever happened. Every church that has been started was first imagined by either a group of people or a church planter. Rarely does something happen until someone starts dreaming.

We need to aspire to become great, godly dreamers. Proverbs 29:18 states, "Where there is no (prophetic foresight), the people cast off restraint (or become unrestrained)." The term "vision" is associated with dreaming, which refers to a type of (sudden revelation), a vision from God. Without this vision, this divine-inspired dreaming, people become "out of control" and lose their ability to exercise self-discipline. When we lack an overarching vision, dream, or goal for our lives, our lives become disordered. Therefore, what we require today are great dreamers.

My prayer is that Acts 2:17 will be true in your life and in your church: "And in the last days it shall be, God declares, that I will pour out my Spirit on all flesh, and your sons and your daughters shall prophesy, and your young men shall see visions, and your old men shall dream dreams."

Let me ask you quite honestly: What's your dream for your next ten years? Have you ever even written it down? Thoughts get untangled once they go through the lips and therefore the fingertips. If you haven't written it down, you haven't really thought about/believed it. Writing makes a person more exact. What's your dream for your family? What's your dream for you personally? How are you getting to change/differ ten years from now?

SOBER

Our church recently embarked on what we call the 'Ten Years of Pre-Planned Future.' We have written down our dreams for the character changes we would like to see in our lives over the next ten years. What would you attempt for God if you knew you could not fail? Today, we are seeking great imaginers.

Each generation needs its C. S. Lewises and J. R. R. Tolkiens, and G. K. Chestertons, and Tolstoys, and Dostoyevskys. We'd like great dreamers, great Imagineering people. Be that where you're. We'd like these in science. We'd like the Boyles. We'd like the Pascals. We'd like the Maxwells in physics and therefore the Keplers and the Calvins. We'd like it in business. We'd like small business starters who dream great dreams and make tons of cash for kingdom purposes.

When I speak of dreaming big dreams, I'm not referring to changing beliefs or ideas. Jude 3 in the Bible states that the faith was 'once for all delivered to the saints,' and the gospel remains unchanging. Attempting to alter it would be ungodly. However, as leaders in the church or our homes, we must acknowledge that what we perceive with our physical eyes is less critical than what we cannot see. As a leader for almost forty years, I can attest to this fact. We can only achieve the impossible if we can envision the invisible.

You may have heard the saying that what the mind can conceive or imagine, the hand can achieve. However, this statement is not entirely accurate. While there is a grain of truth in it, Einstein believed that imagination is more crucial than knowledge because it has no boundaries. Logic can take you from point A to point B, but imagination can take you anywhere. Einstein also claimed that imagination, not knowledge, is the fundamental aspect of intelligence. Similarly, Napoleon famously declared that imagination governs the world. In today's world, we need individuals who can collaborate with like-minded people to create innovative inventions to succeed in future generations. While the message should remain consistent, the methods must evolve with each passing generation.

Innovation

Where does invention of new things come from? The invention of new things often arises from asking the right questions. The only difference between a creative genius and anyone else is that the former asks questions that others don't. Your imagination may be the most significant limitation on your personal growth and your ability to minister to others. If you don't have a dream, God cannot fulfill it. If you don't have his vision for your life, God cannot bless your vision. If you don't have a goal, God cannot assist you in achieving it.

Setting goals can be a powerful expression of faith. As Hebrews 11:6 says, "But without faith it is impossible to please him: for he that cometh to God must believe that he is, and that he is a rewarder of them that diligently seek him." Likewise, Romans 14:23 warns that "he that doubteth is damned if he eat, because he eateth not of faith: for whatsoever is not of faith is sin." According to Matthew 9:29, "according to your faith be it done to you." When we set goals, we are essentially saying to God, "I believe you want me to achieve this, and I trust that with your help, I can reach this by this time." We are challenging and daring God to work with us. I urge you to dream big dreams for God and inspire others to do the same.

Simply refraining from believing everything we expect, protecting our minds from negative influences, and focusing on learning and character development are not enough. We must also allow God to expand our imagination so that we can surpass the world in our thinking, dreaming, and problem-solving abilities, all for the glory of God and the benefit of others, not just for our personal gain.

In Ephesians 3:20, Paul declares, "Now unto him that is able to do exceeding abundantly above all that we ask or think, according to the power that worketh in us." This means that we should reasonably imagine and dream much beyond our highest prayers, desires, thoughts, or hopes. Personally, I consider myself a big dreamer, but God says, "Think of the most important thing you can believe, and I can surpass that. I can exceed that."

A Challenge to Thinkers and to Doers

Many of you are natural thinkers and love the world of thoughts and ideas. You may not necessarily have a deep love for people, but you are passionate about exploring the world of thoughts and ideas. Your idea of growth and ministry may involve staying in your study all week. For some pastors, this could mean spending most of their time preparing for their sermon, and then delivering it from the pulpit before retreating back to their study. This kind of work may be heaven for them.

Maybe you are naturally an excellent thinker -- God wired you that way. And then, there are others who are naturally great doers. They excel in finding ways to bring people to Christ, baptizing them in large numbers, planting churches, preparing servant leaders, helping the poor, caring for the sick, educating future generations, and going out into the hurts, highways, and byways of life to take up the cross where people least expect it. You are a doer.

I would like to have a conversation with you, my friend. I have noticed that those who are natural thinkers often desire to take more action, while those who are natural doers would like to engage in more thinking. However, it is not an "either-or" situation; it is a "both-and" scenario.

Let me leave you with this tiny puzzle-related: THINK. Here are five things to remember in our own lives and to show to others.

"T" stands for test every thought. As stated in Psalms 139:23-24, "Search me, O God, and know my heart! Try me and know my thoughts! And see if there be any grievous way in me, and lead me in the way everlasting!" It is important to ask God to examine and test our thoughts. We should not believe everything that comes to our mind. Instead, we should test every thought and ensure that it aligns with God's truth.

"H" stands for helmet, which protects your head from harm. In California, it is illegal to ride a motorcycle without wearing a helmet. You don't need to wear elbow pads or knee pads, but you must wear a helmet. Why? Because if you injure your head, the consequences can be severe. The Bible also instructs us to "Take the helmet of salvation and the sword of the Spirit, which is the word of God" (Ephesians 6:17), emphasizing the importance of protecting ourselves from harm, both physical and spiritual.

Until we are saved, we don't have any protection against the fiery darts that the Devil unleashes on our minds. Feeling deep sorrow for past sins requires a change of mind, not just a change in behavior. It's primarily a shift in mindset. Feeling deep sorrow for past sins means changing the way you think. It's a mental transformation that leads to putting on the helmet of salvation, which protects us from sin and harm.

"I" stands for Imagine Great Thoughts. Believe in all the good promises of God. "Everything is possible for one who believes." (Mark 9:23). As believers in Christ, we have been given a tremendous privilege and authority. Dare to dream big and imagine great thoughts, anchored in faith in God's promises.

"N" stands for Nourish a Desired Godly Mind. Confirm that you are growing and developing. Psalm 119:15 says, "I will meditate on your precepts and fix my eyes on your ways." Seek to resolve conflicts and establish firm decisions. Study and reflect on God's Word to cultivate a godly mindset.

"K" stands for Keep It Up Learning. The Bible says, "Meditate upon these things; give thyself wholly to them; that thy profiting may appear to all." (1 Timothy 4:15). Are others noticing progress in your life? Are your words and conversations becoming more powerful, meatier, profound, stronger, practical, and life-touching?

The Architecture of the Mind

The human mind is a wonderful and interesting gift from God. While the brain is the physical organ that houses and enables the mind to function within the body, it is through a network called the central nervous system that the mind is able to make sense of the world.

The central nervous system is a complex network of communication that constantly transmits, receives, and interprets billions of chemical and electrical signals between the mind and the physical world around us. It is possible that thinking is a function of interpreting these signals, assigning meaning to them, and ultimately choosing how to respond to them.

For this reason, it is absolutely essential that the "data" we receive is accurate, appropriate, and interpreted correctly. If we receive bad data, our interpretations will be inaccurate, and we will ultimately make wrong decisions. Therefore, we must confirm that we are receiving the correct data, avoid incorrect data, and develop the skills to process and interpret it, resulting in good, God-pleasing decisions that are helpful in living a transformed life.

God and Your Thought Life

God is concerned about our minds. He makes it clear that our thoughts are both visible and significant to Him. Psalm 19:14 states, "Let the words of my mouth and the meditation of my heart be acceptable in your sight, O LORD, my rock and my redeemer," which means that God sees what we harbor in our hearts and minds. Our inner lives can be either acceptable or unacceptable to God. Hebrews 4:13 teaches us that "all things are naked and open to the eyes of Him to whom we must give account." This means that not only does God see our thoughts, but He will hold us accountable for them.

You cannot be held accountable for something over which you have no control. Many of us have bought into the fashionable lie that says, "I can't help what I feel," or that the devil somehow has the ability to control our thought life. People often blame others for their thoughts by saying, "You made me think that." However, if either Satan or people truly had the power to make us feel something, it would be highly unfair for God to hold us responsible for our thoughts. Yet, repeatedly in the Bible, we are not only told what to think, but also that our thought life is our responsibility. This suggests that we can take charge of our own minds, manage our thought life, and choose what we allow to play on the screen of our minds.

That does not mean that we can control every thought that arrives in our mind from the world around us. Every day, thoughts inspired by people, our surroundings, and even evil spirits will come knocking on the door of your mind. These thoughts provoke many feelings that seek to take root in our minds. While we cannot prevent thoughts from coming to the door of our minds, we can choose which thoughts we are going to allow inside. Whether or not we invite a thought inside, entertain it in our mental living room, or let it sleep in a spare bedroom in our heads is entirely up to us. A mentor once said, "Thoughts will come and thoughts will go, but thoughts that are not put into word or action will die— unborn."

Our minds are like the widescreen TV in your home. You cannot choose what the broadcasters will play on a given channel at a given time, but you can choose what channels you are going to allow to play in your home. This is why we must take ownership of our minds and win the battle over the "remote." Because whatever you allow to fill your mind will eventually show up in your life. Proverbs 4:23 says, "Keep your heart with all diligence, for out of it spring the issues of life." Show me your mind, and I will show you your future. You cannot fill your mind with worldly thinking, ungodly entertainment, unclean language and pictures, negative news reports, and fear-filled imaginations, and expect your life to be filled with the blessings and promises of God.

HOPE AND RESILIENCE

The definition of hope can vary depending on the individual discussing it. When people talk about hope in a spiritual context, it may mean believing that good things will happen with faith in a higher power. They may direct their hopes outward in prayer. For others, it may mean always looking on the bright side and seeing challenges as opportunities. Merriam-Webster's definition makes "hope" seem close to "wish": "to cherish a desire with anticipation: to want something to happen or be true." Regardless of the specifics, hope generally means a desire for things to change for the better and to want that better situation very much.

When you're in the clutches of an agonizingly painful situation, it's easy to focus on your suffering and lose sight of the bright ray of hope emerging on the horizon. If your world is falling apart, the difficulties you are experiencing can be overwhelming. Every thought is filtered through a sieve of pain, pressure, and misery. Jeremiah also went through a difficult time, and in Lamentations chapter three, he vividly described how he was feeling, including the one thing that pulled him through: "Just thinking of my troubles and my lonely wandering makes me miserable. That's all I ever think about, and I am depressed. Then I remember something that fills me with hope. The Lord's kindness never fails! If He had not been merciful, we might have been destroyed. The Lord can always be trusted to show mercy every morning. Deep in my heart, I know that 'The Lord is all I need; I can depend on Him!'"

It's understandable that you might feel depressed if you constantly dwell on your troubles. However, if you shift your attention to the God of Hope and reach deep into your heart to say, "The Lord is all I need; I can depend on Him!" - Your pains will be replaced with seeds of heavenly hope that will grow into divine joy, bringing a smile to your soul. Remind yourself that God can use everything in your life for good, even the darkest nights and deepest pains.

"So we're not thrown out." How could we? Although on the surface, it often seems like things are falling apart around us, inside, where God is creating new life, not a day goes by without His unfolding grace. Having hope means expecting an outcome that will make our lives better. It not only helps us endure difficult situations but also inspires us to take the steps necessary to make a better future a reality. Whether we realize it or not, hope is a part of everyone's life. We all hope for something. It's an inherent aspect of being human. Hope helps us define what we want for our futures and is a crucial part of the self-narrative we all have running in our minds about our lives.

Building Resilience

Lately, it seems like the world is lurching from one crisis to another. We have all experienced a global pandemic, dramatic changes to how we conduct our daily lives, economic uncertainty, and political and social turmoil, as well as an array of natural disasters. In addition to these, some people are also dealing with personal traumas such as the loss of a loved one, declining health, unemployment, divorce, violent crime, or tragic accidents. For many of us, this is a time of unprecedented struggle and upheaval.

Whether the source of disruption in your life is a global emergency, a personal tragedy, or both, living through difficult times can have a significant impact on your mood, health, and outlook. It can leave you feeling vulnerable and overwhelmed by stress and anxiety. You may be grieving for what you have lost, experiencing a flood of negative and conflicting emotions, or uncertain about how to move forward with your life. You may even feel like your life is completely out of control, and that you are powerless to influence whatever may happen next.

While there is no way to avoid sorrow, adversity, or distress in life, there are ways to help navigate the rough waters and regain a sense of control. Resilience is the ability to handle loss, change, and trauma, which are inevitable parts of life even before these extraordinary times. Building resilience can help you better adapt to life-changing events, cope with turbulent times, and recover from hardship and tragedy.

Why do some individuals seem better equipped to cope during these troubling times than others? While each person's situation is unique, it is true that individuals with resilience tend to have a higher tolerance for the emotional distress caused by adversity. The more resilient you are, the better you can handle the feelings of stress, anxiety, and sadness that come with trauma and adversity, and find ways to bounce back from setbacks. We all go through tough times, experience disappointment, loss, and change, and feel sad, anxious, and stressed at different points in our lives. However, building resilience can help you maintain a positive outlook, face an uncertain future with less fear, and get through even the darkest days.

If you are more sensitive to emotional distress and finding it challenging to cope with hardship or adversity, it is essential not to consider it as a character flaw. Resilience is not a macho quality and is not fixed; it is an ongoing process that requires effort to develop and maintain over time. Unless you have faced adversity before, it is unlikely that you have had the necessity or opportunity to develop resilience. Drawing on past experiences can assist you in dealing with the challenges you face today. Even if you have struggled to cope with adversity in the past, you may have some experience recognizing coping strategies that do not help, such as attempting to numb your feelings with drugs or alcohol. Although it may be difficult to envision any positives emerging from traumatic experiences, building resilience can assist you in discovering the silver lining within the difficulties you have faced. Surviving hardships can teach you significant things about yourself and the world around you, strengthen your resolve, deepen your empathy, and ultimately enable you to evolve and grow as a human being.

Building resilience can help you stay focused, flexible, and productive in both good and bad times, feel less apprehensive about new experiences or an uncertain future, manage and tolerate strong emotions outside of your comfort zone, including those you'd rather avoid such as anger or despair. Resilience also has the potential to strengthen your relationships and improve your communication skills, particularly during difficult times. It can bolster your self-esteem, allowing you to be confident that you'll eventually find a solution to a problem, even if it's not immediately apparent. You can develop and enhance these qualities of resilience at any time, regardless of your age, background, or circumstances.

STRENGTHENING THE MIND

PRACTICAL WAYS OF BUILDING RESILIENCE

Practice acceptance

While we all react to stressful events in various ways, many people try to protect themselves by refusing to accept the reality of what's happening. Denying that you're experiencing a crisis allows you to deceive yourself that you still have some sense of control over events that are often uncontrollable.

Avoid situational denial

While denial can have some positive functions—for instance, it can offer you a chance to come to terms with the shock of a traumatic event—over time, it will only prolong your pain. Staying in denial will prevent you from adjusting to your new circumstances, hinder you from seeking solutions or taking action, and impede the healing process.

Accept things

Change is an inevitable part of life, and many aspects of the changing world are beyond your personal control. For instance, you can't control the spread of an epidemic, the pace of social change, or how the economy behaves. Although it can be challenging to accept, resisting events or circumstances outside your control will only deplete your energy and leave you feeling anxious and hopeless. On the other hand, accepting your situation can free you up to dedicate your energy to the things that you do have control over.

Focus on things within your control.

Create a list of all the items that are beyond your control and give yourself permission to stop worrying about them. Instead, focus on the actions that you can take. For instance, if you're unemployed, you can't control whether your dream job appears in the classifieds or whether an employer will grant you an interview. However, you can control the amount of time and effort you put into searching for work or brushing up on your skills. Similarly, if a loved one is facing a life-threatening illness, you may have to surrender control to the doctors, but you can still concentrate on providing your loved one with as much emotional support as possible.

Accept your feelings

It can be tempting to believe that the best way to get through adversity is by ignoring painful emotions and "putting on a brave face". However, unpleasant emotions exist whether you choose to acknowledge them or not. Trying to suppress your emotions will only intensify your stress, prolong acceptance of your new situation, and hinder your progress. By allowing yourself to experience your emotions, you will find that even the most intense and upsetting feelings will eventually pass, and the trauma of those tough times will start to fade. This will help you find a way forward. If you're struggling to cope alone, consider asking someone you trust about what you're experiencing or using Help Guide's resources to find support.

Reach others

Connecting with friends and family during tough times can help ease stress, boost your mood, and help you cope with all the changes and disruptions. Rather than feeling like you're facing your problems alone, you can draw strength and build resilience from having others to rely on. The people you reach out to don't have to provide answers to the issues you're facing; they only need to be willing to listen to you without judging. In fact, what you say or the words you use are often unimportant. It's the human connection, such as eye contact, a smile, or a hug, that can make all the difference in how you feel.

Prioritize relationships.

Nothing carries the same health benefits as connecting face-to-face with someone who is caring and empathetic. However, it's not always possible to see friends and loved ones in person, especially if you are separated by geography, lockdown, or travel restrictions. In these situations, you can reach out to others via phone, video chat, or social media. Don't withdraw in tough times. You may be tempted to retreat into your shell when facing challenges in your life. You might fear being a burden to friends and loved ones or feel too exhausted to reach out. But try to continue with social activities even when you don't feel like it. Good friends won't consider you a burden; they're more likely to feel flattered that you trust them enough to open up to them. Try to avoid negative people. Some friends are excellent listeners, kind, and empathetic, while others seem to fuel unconstructive emotions, leaving you feeling even more stressed, anxious, or panicky. Avoid anyone who magnifies your problems, criticizes, or makes you feel judged.

Expand your social network.

Relationships are a vital tool for achieving good mental health, building resilience, and getting through tough times. However, many of us feel that we don't have anyone to turn to in times of need. But there are many ways to create new friendships and improve your support network. If you know of others who are lonely or isolated, take the initiative and reach out to them.

Invest in self-care

Living through tough times can be both mentally and physically draining. Constantly being in a heightened state of stress can cause serious health problems, impact your immune and digestive systems, increase your risk of heart attack and stroke, and lead to burnout - a state of emotional, physical, and mental exhaustion. Since the body and mind are closely linked, investing in self-care is a crucial part of building resilience and getting through times of great stress.

STRENGTHENING THE MIND

When your body feels strong and healthy, your mind will follow suit.

Get enough exercise.

When dealing with chronic stress, it's common to carry it somewhere in your body. You may experience tense muscles, back or neck pain, frequent headaches, insomnia, heartburn, or an upset stomach. Regular exercise not only releases powerful endorphins in the brain to enhance your mood, but it can also help ease tension in the body and counteract the physical symptoms of stress. Practicing a 'mind and body' relaxation technique, such as yoga, tai chi, or meditation, blends deep breathing and body awareness to help you relieve stress and bring your body back to balance.

Improve your sleep.

When you're facing adversity, nothing wears down your resilience like missing out on a good night's sleep. Often, improving your daytime habits and taking the time to relax and unwind before bed can help you sleep better at night. Sleeping naturally revitalizes our body systems, including our thinking faculties. It is a useful tool for relaxation and provides the suitable body condition for proper reflection. Sleeping well can help overcome unwanted thoughts.

Eat well.

There aren't any specific foods that will help build resilience and weather tough times. Rather, it's your overall dietary pattern that's important. Eating a lot of processed and takeout food can take a toll on your brain and mood, sapping your energy and weakening your immune system. On the other hand, a healthy diet - one that's low in sugar and rich in healthy fats - can provide you with the energy and focus to tackle the challenges you're facing.

Look for meaning and purpose

It's easy to become overwhelmed by alarming news headlines or consumed by the crisis you're facing. However, no matter your circumstances, they don't have to define who you are as an individual. You are not your crisis. By engaging in activities that provide purpose and meaning to your life, you can maintain perspective, prevent the situation from overpowering you, and preserve your identity. Since everyone is unique, there are various ways to experience purpose and meaning. Don't confine yourself to the expectations of others; pursue activities that matter to you and bring satisfaction to your life.

Give help to others.

When you're in the midst of a crisis, it's common to experience feelings of powerlessness and helplessness. However, by taking proactive steps to help others, you can regain a sense of control and purpose in your life. In fact, providing support can be just as beneficial as receiving it. Consider volunteering with organizations, assisting people in your community, donating blood, contributing to a charity, or participating in a protest for a cause that holds significance for you.

Pursue your hobbies and interests.

During turbulent times, it's crucial not to abandon the interests that nourish your spirit. For many of us, these pursuits define us as individuals and bring meaning to our lives. Whether it's engaging in sports, caring for a pet, pursuing artistic or musical endeavors, undertaking home improvement projects, or spending time in nature, continuing to derive pleasure from your hobbies and passions can enhance your ability to cope with the stress of difficult times.

Stay motivated

An essential aspect of coping with adversity and navigating tough times is cultivating qualities of persistence and endurance. Challenging circumstances are typically not permanent, and by their very definition, they eventually come to an end. As you chart a path through the darkness, it's crucial to find ways to stay motivated and persevere.

Handle the problems structurally – A step at a time.

If a problem feels too overwhelming to tackle all at once, try breaking it down into smaller, more manageable steps. Even if you can't immediately see a solution, you can take action by creating a list, researching more about the topic, or seeking the advice of a trusted friend or loved one.

Celebrate small wins.

To maintain motivation and a positive outlook as you navigate difficult times in life, take a moment to celebrate your small successes. For example, if you are searching for work, getting an interview may not be as significant as landing a job, but it is a sign of progress and a step in the right direction. Recognizing these small wins can provide a much-needed break from the stress and negativity you are facing, and inspire you to keep pushing forward.

Try to maintain a hopeful outlook.

While it can be challenging to maintain a positive and hopeful outlook during a crisis, many of us have a tendency to exaggerate our problems and make them seem even more negative than they actually are. To combat this, try stepping back and examining your situation as an outsider. Are there any positive aspects that you can focus on? Instead of worrying about what you fear might happen, try visualizing what you would like to happen instead.

Express gratitude.

It may sound cliche, but even during times of great difficulty, it's often possible to find something to be grateful for - like the love of a pet, a beautiful sunset, or a caring friend. Taking a moment to acknowledge your gratitude for these small things can provide a respite from stress and significantly boost your mood.

STRENGTHENING THE MIND

Be kind to yourself.

Everyone adjusts to change and upheaval differently. Don't criticize your coping skills or beat yourself up for any mistakes you make. Self-compassion is a crucial part of building resilience, so be kind to yourself.

CHAPTER EIGHT

THE POWER OF MEDITATION

Thomas Hooker said, "Meditation is a serious intention of the mind whereby we search out the truth and settle it effectively upon the heart." In Swami Muktananda's words, "Your goal is not to battle with the mind but to witness the mind." Meditation gives individuals the power to ascertain facts and discover their purposes. Scripture also shows us the power of meditation both to God and ourselves. For example, "Let the words of my mouth and the meditation of my heart be acceptable in Your sight, O LORD, my strength and my Redeemer" (Psalm 19:14), "This Book of the Law shall not depart from your mouth, but you shall meditate in it day and night, that you may observe to do according to all that is written in it. For then you will make your way prosperous, and then you will have good success" (Joshua 1:8), and "My eyes are awake through the night watches, that I may meditate on Your word" (Psalm 119:148).

Believe it or not, the Bible actually teaches us to meditate. However, the practice of biblical meditation is quite different from the meditation taught by gurus and religions in the Far East. In those religions, meditation is taught as the emptying of the mind. But the Bible never tells us to empty our minds! Instead, we are encouraged to fill our minds with His Word. Biblical meditation is the practice of focusing our minds on Jesus, the wonderful promises He has made to us, and the teachings of the Bible. While many non-Christian philosophies teach that meditation is a skill that takes years to master, the simple truth is that meditation is a practice that we all engage in every day of our lives.

HEART "SOUNDS"

Meditation is simply the practice of focused thinking. It comes from several Hebrew root words. In Psalm 19:14, the word "meditate" comes from the word "*higgäyon*," which means to repeatedly strike the string of a harp to make a lasting sound. It is also used in these other passages:

"Upon an instrument of ten strings, and upon the psaltery; upon the harp with a solemn sound." (Psalm 92:3 KJV). The LORD is known by the judgment which he executeth: the wicked is snared in the work of his own hands. Higgaion. Selah (Psalm 9:16.)

The word translated as "heart" in Psalm 19:14 is "leb." It's the Hebrew word for the core of one's soul, thought, imagination, and memory. These two words form a strong image of what happens when we focus our innermost thoughts on a specific idea or thing. David was actually praying that the sounds of his mind would be acceptable in the sight of God.

THE POWER OF MEDITATION

When we believe something for an extended period of time, we create a "sound" in our minds. This sound has a way of dominating our perspective of life, eventually making us sensitive to things that have a similar "tone." Positive or negative, right or wrong, blessing or cursing, the focus of our meditations will begin to attract people, circumstances, and feelings that are tuned to that same pitch. And anything we meditate on long enough will try to control our thinking, impact the direction of our choices, and become our experience. Whatever we expect over time, we start to attract. Our minds begin to draw associations and reinforce beliefs that cause us to fixate on the things we expect. This is why it's so important to develop the right meditations. Whatever occupies your mind will eventually occupy your life!

As previously stated, each one of us meditates every day. In our spare moments, while driving to work, or silently waiting in line, our minds drift towards the dominant patterns of thinking we have established. These are not empty thoughts! These meditations of our hearts are strongly impacting the way we experience life and they are putting forth their particular sound—either attracting or repelling us from the promises of God. One of the best ways to see how we use the power of our minds to meditate every day is by observing the things we worry about.

SOBER

DEFEATING THE FEAR HABIT

The Bible has a lot to say about the negative impact of worry in our lives. Worry is the practice of negative meditation. Note what Jesus and Paul taught about the worry habit:

"Therefore I say to you, do not worry about your life" (Matthew 6:25).

"Therefore do not worry, saying, 'What shall we eat?' or 'What shall we drink?' or 'What shall we wear?'" (Matthew 6:31).

"Therefore do not worry about tomorrow, for tomorrow will worry about its own things. Sufficient for the day is its own trouble" (Matthew 6:34).

Worrying is imagining the future in a negative way. We don't worry about things that have already happened — only things that we fear might happen. Worry pictures the bills going unpaid, the promotion at work passing us by, or the pain in our chest becoming a heart attack. When we worry, we give the power of our minds to imagine the worst possible outcome in every situation. Worry destroys faith. We become focused on our fears rather than God's plans and the possibilities He offers for our lives. Worry keeps us trapped in fear and avoidance. It never solves or resolves anything! This is why the Bible tells us to replace our worried imaginations with focused prayer requests. Instead of letting our fears and problems stew in our minds, we are to take action by bringing

THE POWER OF MEDITATION

them to God in prayer. Only God has the power to change our circumstances. When we pray, God comes to our aid. He exchanges our fear and worry for His peace in our minds, and our weakness in the face of our trouble transforms into a strong and renewed faith in God's sovereign plan for us.

For instance, instead of fretting over an upcoming bill or a negative report, view the matter as an opportunity to exercise your faith through prayer. God is already aware of the situation, so take this time to speak His Word over it. As you do so, seek God's guidance, wisdom, direction, or healing. Infuse your prayer with genuine gratitude, and it will unleash the power of the Holy Spirit over your situation. By applying this practical technique, your faith can triumph over fear and break negative thinking patterns that keep you trapped in fear and hinder your growth. Paul offers a potent remedy for the fear habit by urging us to redirect our focus from anticipating the worst to anticipating God's solution!

"Don't worry about anything; instead, pray about everything. Tell God what you would like, and thank him for all he has done. Then you'll experience God's peace, which exceeds anything we will understand. His peace will guard your hearts and minds as you reside in Christ Jesus" (Philippians 4:6-7 NLT).

The outcome of right thinking is always God's perfect peace. One way to determine if your thought life is moving in the right direction is by assessing your peace level. If your thoughts are focused on God, His Word, and you trust Him with your problems, you will experience genuine inner peace. This peace is not dependent on having a perfect life or all your circumstances being favorable. Rather, it arises from relying on the Lord in your mind. This peace remains constant, irrespective of your circumstances. The prophet Isaiah confirms this in his book, where he says, "You will keep in perfect and constant peace the one whose mind is steadfast [that is, committed and focused on You—in both inclination and character], Because he trusts and takes refuge in You [with hope and confident expectation]" (Isaiah 26:3 AMP).

A FOOD FOR YOUR MIND

Just as the food you consume shapes your body, the thoughts you feed your mind and emotions shape your mental and emotional health. Therefore, it is crucial that we carefully select a diet of God's Word for our minds. Initially, it may be challenging to limit our intake of negative thoughts, unhealthy images, and pessimistic attitudes. However, if we focus on the following list and nourish our minds with thoughts, images, and relationships that promote them, we can develop a healthy and robust mind. Here is the list:

"And now, dear brothers and sisters, one final thing. Fix your thoughts on what is true, and honorable, and right, and pure, and lovely, and admirable. Think about things that are excellent and worthy of praise. Keep putting into practice all you learned and received from me—

everything you heard from me and saw me doing. Then the God of peace will be with you" Philippians 4:8 (NLT).

Paul offers us eight categories of mental nourishment to guide our thinking. We should subject every tempting thought to the filter of these categories. If a thought fails to meet the criteria, we should reject it and replace it with thoughts that do. This way, we can ensure that our minds are constantly nourished with healthy and positive thoughts.

Paul's Mind Diet:

Paul outlines eight categories of mental food that we should focus on to guide our thoughts:

1. Truthful Things: Our thoughts must be rooted in real facts that are grounded in Scripture. Anything contrary to truth, such as lies or deception, must be rejected.
2. Honorable Things: Our thoughts should show respect towards God, others, and ourselves. We should think honorably towards our loved ones, leaders, and authorities.
3. Righteous Things: Our minds must focus on things that reflect righteousness, justice, and God's kingdom.
4. Pure Things: We should not allow any morally impure or polluted thoughts to enter our minds, including those related to sexual impurity.
5. Lovely Things: We should think about beautiful sights, sounds, and relationships, and avoid anything that is ugly or unattractive.

6. Admirable Things: We should seek out people and things that inspire admiration within us and focus our attention on them.

7. Excellent Things: Our minds need a high-quality diet, focusing on things that challenge us to rise above mediocrity and reach our potential.

8. Praiseworthy Things: Focusing on things we can thank and praise God for helps defeat negative thinking habits. Whenever our mind drifts towards negativity, we should immediately think of something to thank and praise God for, voicing our gratitude and allowing ourselves to feel thankful. This action alone has a powerful effect on resetting our minds and breaking negative thinking cycles.

CHAPTER NINE

YOU MUST BE SOBER

"Let us not sleep, as others do, but let us watch and be sober. For those who sleep, sleep at night, and those who get drunk are drunk at night. But let us who are of the day be sober" (1 Thessalonians 5:6-8).

What does it mean to be sober? Sobriety is the opposite of intoxication or drunkenness. In the New Testament, the term 'be sober' means to be free from all forms of intoxication, whether physical or spiritual. Someone under the influence is confused in their thinking, unable to think straight, and tends to underestimate risks and dangers. While there are varying degrees of intoxication, being sober is absolute. Sobriety is the absence of intoxication.

In 1 Peter 1:13, the phrase "Gird up the loins of your mind, be sober" is used. The expression "gird up your loins" means to be ready for action. Therefore, we must be mentally prepared and alert, which requires sobriety.

The command to be sober is an important aspect of sound doctrine, as emphasized in Paul's message to Timothy: "But speak thou the things which become sound doctrine: That the aged men be sober, grave, temperate, sound in faith, in charity, in patience. The aged women likewise, that they be in behavior as becometh holiness, not false accusers, not given to much wine, teachers of good things;" (Titus 2:1-3).

Older men should be sober, and older women should not be enslaved to alcohol. Although this verse is specifically directed towards the elderly, it applies to everyone. To be enslaved means to be subdued by something, and someone who is addicted to alcohol may require a specific amount of it every day. Alcohol is a habit-forming drug that depresses bodily functions and dulls the mind.

In order to be appointed as an elder, a person should not be addicted to wine (1 Timothy 3:3; Titus 1:7). Addiction involves an overwhelming urge to use a drug because the body has developed a chemical dependence, often accompanied by a psychological dependence. Painful and distressing withdrawal symptoms can occur if the habitual amount is not obtained.

A habit-forming drug can cause changes in body chemistry that trigger compensating reactions in an effort to restore degraded functions. For example, alcohol depresses the central nervous system and slows down bodily functions, including heart rate and general sensitivity. In response, the body compensates by speeding up the heart and increasing sensitivity. Even after the alcohol is metabolized by the liver, the compensatory effects may persist for some time. This can make a person feel tense, anxious, and hypersensitive, which can lead to cravings for alcohol to offset these feelings.

YOU MUST BE SOBER

Alcohol is a mood-changing drug that has a relaxing effect, reduces inhibitions, and creates a false sense of security and well-being. Due to the body's compensatory reactions, however, one must continually consume more alcohol to achieve the same effects. Since the pleasant effects only occur while the alcohol content in the blood is rising and reverses as the alcohol level drops, the use of alcohol can easily become a vicious circle of increasing compulsive use. As the Bible says in Hosea 4:11, 'Whoredom and wine and new wine take away the heart.' Different substances have different levels of addictiveness, and different individuals may react to addictive substances in different ways.

Christians are instructed to be sober, therefore we must avoid intoxication and addiction to alcohol. However, does this mean that a Christian should never consume anything that contains even a small amount of alcohol?

According to the New Testament, Jesus drank wine. In Luke 7:33-35 and Matthew 11:18-19, it is written, "For John the Baptist came neither eating bread nor drinking wine, and you say, 'He features a demon.' The Son of Man has not come for eating and drinking, and you say, 'Look, a glutton and a winebibber, a lover of tax collectors and sinners!'" Although these accusations were false, Jesus did drink wine, and He was not a glutton or a drunkard.

Wine was a common beverage in Biblical times. The term 'wine' referred to both fermented and unfermented fruit juice. Fruit juice was preserved by both fermentation and boiling, which reduced it to half or one-third of its original volume, resulting in an unfermented concentrated juice that could be stored for several years.

In modern times, the alcohol content of most wines is typically increased by adding sugar during fermentation. Fortified wines, such as Port and Sherry, have additional alcohol added to them directly.

In ancient times, it was customary to dilute wine by adding two or three parts water to one part wine. By doing so, Jews followed the Old Testament warnings against strong drink (Proverbs 20:1; Isaiah 5:11).

The wording in Revelation 14:10 is related to the present practice of making strong wines: "He himself shall also drink of the wine of the wrath of God, which is poured out full strength into the cup of His indignation." In some translations, the phrase "poured out unmixed" is used instead of "full strength".

The practice of diluting wine is supported by modern research, as alcohol can have damaging effects on various parts of the body, including the skin, brain, liver, and heart. In fact, high levels of alcohol in the bloodstream (0.4 percent or higher) can even lead to death.

Mnesitheus, an Athenian medical doctor in the fourth century BC, described wine as follows: "In life, to those who mix and drink it moderately, it gives good cheer. But if you overstep the bounds, it brings violence. Mix it in part, and you get madness! Unmixed, bodily collapse!" Similarly, Eubulus, an Athenian writer and statesman of the same era, warned that harm comes to those who drink wine stronger than a ratio of three parts wine to nine parts water.

Thus, the wine that Jesus used had much less alcohol than most wine in the market today.

Those who aspire to follow Jesus' example should remember that He never sinned. The Bible teaches us that Jesus "can sympathize with our weaknesses" because He was "tempted in every way, just as we are, yet He did not sin" (Hebrews 4:15). Given that the Bible instructs us to be sober and condemns both drunkenness and addiction, we can infer that Jesus never consumed excessive amounts of wine, nor was He addicted to it.

Timothy, who previously drank no wine, was encouraged by Paul to use a touch wine for medicinal purposes: "No longer drink only water, but use a touch wine for your stomach's sake and your frequent infirmities" (1 Timothy 5:23).

From this, we may conclude that it's not a sin to drink small amounts of wine as long together remains completely sober and isn't addicted.

The Scriptures also teach that there are situations where it is appropriate to refrain from drinking altogether. Under the Old Covenant, priests were forbidden from drinking wine while on duty: "Do not drink wine nor strong drink, you, nor your sons with you, when you go into the tabernacle of meeting, lest you die. It shall be a statute forever throughout your generations, that you may make a distinction between holy and unholy, and between unclean and clean, and that you may teach the children of Israel all the statutes which the Lord has spoken to them by the hand of Moses" (Leviticus 10:9-11). Similarly, the book of Ezekiel states that "No priest shall drink wine when he enters the inner court" (Ezekiel 44:21).

Although this is not a law, we should always consider the extent to which the reasoning and principles behind this Old Testament restriction might still apply to church leaders under the New Covenant.

People in important positions shouldn't drink. "It is not for kings, O Lemuel, it is not for kings to drink wine; nor for princes strong drink: they drink, and forget the law, and pervert the judgment of any of the afflicted." (Proverbs 31:4, 5).

In our current era, this advice is relevant to anyone who operates a vehicle. Even non-religious individuals promote responsible driving by advocating against drunk driving with the slogan, "If you've had a drink, let someone else drive.

There are also health concerns to consider. The American Medical Association advises pregnant women to avoid drinking any amount of alcoholic beverages, as even small amounts of alcohol in the mother's bloodstream can cause brain damage to the developing fetus. It is important to note that women are more sensitive to alcohol than men due to their lower blood volume. On average, half a glass of wine puts the same amount of alcohol into a woman's bloodstream as a whole glass does for a man. Furthermore, some studies suggest that alcohol use by fathers can also lead to brain damage in their children.

As their brains are still developing, alcohol can also cause brain damage to children and adolescents. Therefore, the American Medical Association recommends that no one under the age of 21 should consume any amount of alcohol.

Certain medications, including many painkillers, should not be mixed with alcohol. In addition, even small amounts of alcohol can trigger migraines and panic attacks in some individuals, particularly after the effects of alcohol wear off.

Some individuals may choose to abstain from alcohol altogether, as anyone can develop alcohol dependency. However, certain individuals are particularly susceptible to alcoholism, which is an incurable condition. It's estimated that between 5 to 7% of the population are active alcoholics, while the percentage of latent alcoholics is difficult to determine but believed to be similar at 5 to 7%. Latent alcoholics have not yet developed alcohol dependency, but due to their makeup, they may become addicted if they consume alcohol.

Studies have found that an alcoholic's body can quickly adapt to the effects of alcohol, which may allow them to consume alcohol without appearing intoxicated. However, this rapid adjustment also leads to a quick dependence and addiction, as the body begins to rely on alcohol once the individual starts drinking. Gradually, more and more alcohol is needed to prevent distressing withdrawal symptoms, creating a vicious cycle. Unless the individual accepts that the only solution for them is complete abstinence from alcohol, their health and life can be destroyed by alcoholism.

Alcoholism can manifest in various ways, with compulsive use of alcohol being either continuous or periodic. Some alcoholics may begin by drinking small amounts of alcohol each day, and although they may not appear drunk initially, the amount they consume gradually increases over time. Eventually, the alcohol in their bloodstream begins to interfere with their personal, family, social, and professional activities.

Some alcoholics can go without drinking for a day, but once they have a single drink, they are unable to prevent themselves from having another, and then another. Although the negative consequences of excessive drinking may cause them to abstain from alcohol for a short period of time, the same pattern repeats itself the next time they feel the need to drink.

The causes of alcoholism are complex, and there are several underlying factors, including a genetic element. Research has shown that while the general population has a 10-15% chance of developing alcoholism, the child of an alcoholic has a 25% chance of being highly vulnerable to it. It is not shameful to have this hereditary susceptibility, but someone who does should be prepared to accept the fact that they must avoid alcohol entirely to prevent addiction.

Some of the initial warning signs of alcoholism include needing a particular amount of alcohol every day, intending to take only one drink but ending up consuming several, having a craving and enthusiasm for alcoholic beverages, drinking before stressful situations, having a drink to calm one's nerves, drinking alone, having a drink in the morning, neglecting responsibilities to buy alcohol, becoming more accident-prone, hiding the amount of alcohol consumed from family and friends, and denying that there is a problem when others suggest that too much alcohol is being consumed

Denial is a common behavior, even in advanced stages of alcoholism. The individual struggling with alcohol addiction may not think clearly about their alcohol use. Additionally, loved ones may also be in denial and make excuses for the alcoholic's behavior.

Christians must be sober. We might not befuddle our minds with alcohol or be hooked in to alcohol.

"Thus be alert in your thinking, be sober" (1 Peter 1:13 RD).

Avoiding alcohol abuse can be a matter of life and death, both physically and spiritually. Alcohol has been responsible for destroying numerous lives and turning many homes into a living hell. In addition to causing thousands of deaths annually from alcohol poisoning and alcohol-related illnesses like liver failure, alcohol is involved in 50% of arrests,

SOBER

40% of traffic fatalities, 30% of fire fatalities, 30% of drowning incidents, and 20% of suicides. As it says in 1 Peter 5:8, 'Be sober, be vigilant, because your adversary the devil walks about like a roaring lion, seeking whom he may devour.

Let us remain sober and watchful, like those who stay awake. For those who sleep, do so at night, and those who get drunk, do so at night as well. But let us who belong to the day, be sober, as it says in 1 Thessalonians 5:6-8. Amen.

CONCLUSION

GOD'S PURPOSE: PEACE AND LIFE

God loves you and needs you to experience peace and life – abundant and eternal. "We have peace with God through our Lord Jesus Christ." (Romans 5:1)" For God so loved the world that He gave His only begotten Son, that whoever believes in Him should not perish but have everlasting life." (John 3:16)

OUR PROBLEM: SEPARATION AND DEATH

God created us in His own image to live an abundant life. He did not create us as robots to automatically love and obey Him, but gave us a will and freedom of choice. Since the beginning of humanity, people have chosen to disobey God and go their own way. We still make this choice today, which leads to eternal separation from God. As it says in Romans 3:23, 'For all have sinned and fall short of the glory of God.' The wages of sin is death, but the gift of God is eternal life in Christ Jesus our Lord, as stated in Romans 6:23.

OUR ATTEMPTS

Throughout the ages, people have attempted in various ways to bridge the gap between themselves and God, but without success. Intoxication or drunkenness is not the solution to this problem Those human attempt has failed and repeatedly continue to fail. "But your iniquities have separated you from God; and your sins have hidden His face from you, so that He will not hear." (Isaiah 59:2)

GOD'S REMEDY: THE CROSS

Jesus Christ is the only solution to this problem. He died on the Cross and rose from the grave, paying the penalty for our sins and bridging the gap between God and us. As it says in 1 Peter 3:18a, 'For Christ also suffered once for sins, the just for the unjust, that He might bring us to God.' And in Romans 5:8, 'But God demonstrates His own love for us in this: While we were still sinners, Christ died for us.

OUR RESPONSE: RECEIVE CHRIST

We must trust Jesus and invite Him into our lives personally. Then, by being sober, we put on the helmet of salvation which helps our minds focus on heaven. As it says in Revelation 3:20, 'Behold, I stand at the door and knock. If anyone hears My voice and opens the door, I will come in to him and dine with him, and he with Me.' And in Romans 10:9, 'If you confess with your mouth that Jesus is Lord and believe in your heart that God raised Him from the dead, you will be saved.

HOW TO RECEIVE CHRIST

Is there any good reason why you can't receive Jesus right now?

Admit your need. ("I am a sinner.")

Be willing to show away from your sins (repent).

CONCLUSION

Believe that Jesus died for you on the Cross and he rose from the grave.

Through prayer, we can invite Jesus to come into our lives and guide us through the Holy Spirit. We receive Him as our Lord and Savior. Here is an example prayer:

Dear Lord Jesus, I know that I am a sinner and I ask for Your forgiveness. I believe that You died for my sins and I want to turn away from them. I invite You to come into my heart and life. I want to trust and follow You as my Lord and Savior. In Jesus' name, Amen.

GOD'S ASSURANCE: HIS WORD

If you have prayed this prayer sincerely, the Bible gives assurance that you will be saved through Christ and spend eternity with Him in Heaven. Upon receiving Christ, we are born into God's family through the supernatural work of the Holy Spirit who indwells every believer. This is called regeneration or the "new birth." "For it is by grace you have been saved, through faith – and this is not from yourselves, it is the gift of God – not by works, so that no one can boast" (Ephesians 2:8-9). "He who has the Son has life; he who does not have the Son of God does not have life. These things I have written to you who believe in the name of the Son of God, that you may know that you have eternal life, and that you may continue to believe in the name of the Son of God" (1 John 5:12-13).

Resume: This book is About the helmet of Salvation, *put it on keep it on*. In nine chapter you will learn how to master your mind. Also, the book emphasizes the limitations of using alcohol as a coping mechanism and highlights the benefits of sobriety, both for those struggling with addiction and for those seeking to improve their overall well-being. It acknowledges that the journey towards sobriety can be intimidating and challenging, but it is necessary to confront the underlying issues in order to achieve long-term recovery.

"Most of us were born into this world headfirst, emerging from the womb. Similarly, to escape from challenging circumstances, professional limitations, or stagnation in your ministry, you need to lead with your head. Don't lose your mind." Overall, the book promotes the idea of facing difficult problems head-on and encourages individuals to consider the positive changes that can result from living a sober lifestyle.

Author: *Pastor Sam is a Preacher, Motivator, Author, he is also one of the most coveted faith-based influencers in Business, Education, and Social Development. He has counseled Pastors, politicians and entrepreneurs, he is Founder, President, and Senior Pastor of Kingdom Colony Ministries, base in Fall River, Massachusetts in United States of America Pastor Sam is a Church planter, International Motivational Speaker and Business Consultant.*

www.ingramcontent.com/pod-product-compliance
Lightning Source LLC
Chambersburg PA
CBHW060509290526
45791CB00001B/331